CW00797787

FOR

THE

LOVE

OF

COOKIES

FOR
THE
LOVE
OF
COOKIES

MARILYN ALICE TUCKMAN

atmosphere press

This book is dedicated to my darling husband Jeff.

He has tremendous patience with himself and —thankfully—with me, too.

AND

In loving memory of "Auntie" Adeline

CONTENTS

Mom, Me, and Pepper

INTRODUCTION

When my brother Frank and I were kids, Mom let us play with her floured pastry cloth. She made homemade egg noodles. The dough was rolled paper thin on the cloth and then transferred to a big cutting board. Mom cut the dough into diagonal strips and let them dry on our kitchen table. The noodles were off limits, but Mom let us do things with the pastry cloth. Frank rolled his toy cars in the flour to make tire tracks and arranged toy soldiers on a floured battlefield.

After he had his fill of this, I'd smooth the cloth with a pancake turner and press cookie cutters all over to see how many shapes I could get out of the surface.

Frank and I were blessed with parents who let us get messy and dirty. As a little girl, I was allowed to make back-yard mud pies. Surprisingly, I remained quite tidy and my sun-baked pies were beautiful. The ingredients included just me, the earth, water and sunshine. Such unleashed experiences gave me a way to express myself without interference or instruction.

Playtime had a sacred quality; it was enthralling.

As a girl, collecting recipes came naturally to me, and organizing them into categories was one of my favorite pastimes. I loved cookbooks with pictures and spent many afternoons looking through one of my most treasured books—Better Homes & Gardens Barbecue Book (1956). I did this with my dog Pepper beside me, pointing out and explaining the pictures to him. Actually, reading to Pepper is how I finally learned how to read; I didn't read or spell well in school. Today, I still have my beautifully illustrated and deeply cherished barbecue book. It continues to inspire me to this day, as it rekindles warm memories of Pepper.

The cookie recipes in this cookbook include my own personal favorites. They're recipes that have been the most successful for me and most enthusiastically enjoyed by family, friends and neighbors over the course of decades, in many cases. Although, I've added a collection of flour-free recipes (pages 189 to 212) because some of my loved ones have stopped eating wheat flour in recent times. In their interest, I searched for and adapted what I've found to be one dozen delicious flour-free recipes.

Finally, this book is inspired by "Auntie" Adeline. Adeline was my mother's oldest and dearest friend, a serious cookie baker, and a great lady to share a pot of tea with on a cold winter afternoon. I have wonderful memories of drinking tea with Adeline and eating our leftover homemade cookies a day or two after Christmas—just the two of us in her tiny kitchen comparing cookies and sharing recipes. We did this during the few years following Mom's passing and before Adeline passed over, too. The ritual gave me comfort and the budding idea for a future cookie cookbook. Here it is!

I hope you will dig deeply into the recipes and enjoy the cookies.

Sincerely,

Marilyn Alice Tuckman

INGREDIENT NOTES

Baking truly delicious cookies from scratch can be challenging; lots of variables are open to mishaps. Using the right ingredients in the first place increases success odds. This is so true for flavorings.

EXTRACTS

There is no substitution for 100% pure extracts. **Skip any imitation flavorings**; they are chemically harsh and barely represent the real essence of a natural flavor. Vanilla is my favorite and most used extract in this book, followed by almond. When pure, vanilla appeals to just about everyone.

Rum and maple extracts can complement recipes with a lovely scent and flavor. For example, either can be used in *Maple Walnut Bars* (page 116), and rum extract in combo with espresso powder is fabulous in *Rum-Espresso Cookies* (page 40). However, these extracts are not totally pure; they are made with a combination of other flavors. In such cases, buy extracts that tout only natural and no artificial flavors.

Pure orange and lemon extracts are found in just one recipe, *Sunny Citrus Cookies* (page 90). Several other recipes include lemon or orange flavor, but the flavoring is provided by the zest of the fruit—not an extract. Zest is a very important flavor ingredient and is addressed on page XIII.

Pure peppermint extract is delightful and appears in *Peppermint Stars* (page 42) and is suggested as an idea in *Coconut Meringues* (page 206).

SPICES

I adore the home-associated, warm-brown spices including cinnamon, nutmeg, allspice, ginger, clove and cardamom. They appear here-and-there in the recipes, some more than others. Their aromas and tastes work together in wonderful combinations. *Spicy Butter Cookies* (page 30) is a beautiful example of warm spices in perfect balance.

I buy ground spices of varying quality to taste and compare, including store brands and organic.

More importantly, I always check the **"best used by"** date on the container to make sure the spice is potent and flavorful. My best advice is to check the dates on spice bottles in your pantry—often—to make sure they're fresh. Buy spices in quantities that you're able to use up within a few months. Also, store spices in a cool-dark place—away from your stove top and oven.

BUTTER, OIL, SHORTENING & COOKING SPRAY

Unsalted butter is used throughout this book in recipes that call for butter. It allows better control over the amount of salt used in a recipe. If salted butter is all you have on hand, omit any salt that's included among the ingredients. Actually, many recipes have no salt nor need for it.

Do not substitute margarine for butter. Unless a recipe specifically calls for margarine or allows it as an option, don't use it. The majority of cookies in this book are "butter cookies" and depend on true buttery richness for their outstanding flavor. Never use whipped or light butter; they contain added air and water and are not suitable for baking.

Vegetable shortening is used in several recipes, especially among cookies from the 1970's in the "Year-Round Favorites" section. I've tried doing a butter replacement for several of these cookies, but found the changes in texture undesirable. So, I leave you with the original, unaltered recipes. If you insist on using butter, do a 50% replacement—half butter, half shortening.

"Butter-flavored" shortening is specifically called for in a few recipes while other recipes use plain shortening, but they are interchangeable. Both shortenings mix well with the large amount of sugar used in cookie recipes. However, "butter-flavored" shortening (claimed to be naturally and artificially flavored) will contribute "something" to the overall taste of your cookies.

Oil appears as an ingredient in only a few recipes. I recommend using canola oil first and corn oil second. Canola oil is light and neutral tasting. Corn oil is heavier; and, as it ages, it takes on the aroma and flavor of its source—corn. Still, it's one of the most commonly used oils and a good all-purpose ingredient when fresh. Be sure to store oils in a cool-dark place to prolong freshness. Canola and corn oil store well in the refrigerator when used within a few months.

Cooking spray is a kitchen staple. Whether its source is canola, corn, olives or a blend, it's good for quickly greasing baking pans. Although, lightly plying cookie sheets with butter is better; golden-buttery crusts add to the flavor and appeal of homemade cookies.

A really good use for cooking spray is for flattening balls of dough. Use the spray to grease the bottom of a drinking glass before it's dipped into granulated sugar and then pressed over dough balls. Sugar adheres well to the sprayed surface, and just the right amount of sugar transfers to the dough.

SUGARS

Yes, cookies are sugary, so two things: First, I use no imitation sweeteners; and, second, I keep on hand granulated, powdered, light-brown and dark-brown sugars. I also keep turbinado "raw" sugar, decorative sugars, and jimmies stashed in an airtight canister in my pantry.

Granulated white sugar is used in most of the recipes in this book, sometimes in combination with other sugars. It lasts indefinitely, so I buy large bags and transfer the sugar to glass Mason jars. My advice is to avoid buying a bag with hard lumps inside. Before purchasing, squeeze the bag and try to feel if the sugar is loose. Lumpy sugar is very annoying when you're ready to bake.

Light and dark-brown sugars are used abundantly in the recipes. Both contain molasses, the light having less than the dark. Either light or dark sugar is often specified in recipes, but they are interchangeable—with a notable flavor difference. Dark-brown sugar has more of the robust, complex-organic flavor of molasses. This stronger flavor is quite powerful and truly enhances certain cookies such as *No-Bake Peanut Butter Oat Squares* (page 210) and *Toasted Almond Drops* (page 176). A few recipes let you choose the sugar. For example, *Whole-Wheat Oatmeal Cookies* (page 70) is a recipe that's delicious when made with either light or dark sugar or a combo of both.

So, when it comes to making cookies, the use of light or dark-brown sugar is really a matter of taste—or strength of the molasses flavor.

Powdered sugar (also known as confectioners' or 10X sugar) is pulverized granulated sugar mixed with a little cornstarch to prevent clumping. It's used as an ingredient to make dough, icings and frostings. Sometimes hot cookies are rolled in it to coat allover. The sugar melts on the hot surface and turns into a thick sweet frosting. Powdered sugar is often lightly dusted over finished cookies, too. Use a fine-mesh sieve (a strainer) for dusting; it adds air and lightness to the sugar.

Fine granulated sugar is needed to make *Cocoa Meringue Kisses* (page 208). Fine sugar is granulated sugar with uncommonly small crystals. It's used when a faster dissolving granule is needed and produces a finer textured meringue than what's possible with ordinary granulated sugar.

FLOURS

Most of the recipes in this book use **all-purpose flour**, both bleached and unbleached are acceptable. However, bleached flour produces a more tender cookie with a more refined, less wheat-like taste.

Don't use **self-rising flour**; it already contains leavening and salt. For recipes that use **whole-wheat flour**, it's okay to substitute all-purpose, but don't replace all-purpose with whole-wheat. Whole-wheat flour lacks sufficient gluten and will produce cookies that are coarsely textured. If you want to use whole-wheat flour, replace no more than 50% of all-purpose with whole-wheat.

Two recipes use **cake flour**, *Cinnamon Snowballs* (page 18) and *Pecan Puffs* (page 84). This flour is more finely milled than all-purpose and is lighter, finer and softer. Cake flour gives these cookies a soft, tender texture. For best results, don't substitute another flour.

I love **almond flour** for two good reasons. First, it can replace ground almonds in recipes that call for grinding the hard nuts, see *Chinese New-Year Nut Balls* (page 104). I use "raw" almond flour because it retains the brown skin of the nut and is beautifully speckled. It adds an appealing textured appearance to baked goods, especially cookies.

A second good reason to love almond flour is that it can sometimes replace wheat flour. Three recipes that do this deliciously are *Gluten-Free Lemon Almond Cookies* (page 196), *Gluten-Free Coconut Drops* (page 198), and *My Favorite Granola Bars* (page 212).

Another alternative for wheat flour is **sorghum flour.** Sorghum is best known as a thick sweet syrup, but it's actually a type of grass that's cultivated as a grain and ground into a flour. Sorghum is used as a gluten-free flour along with **xanthan gum** (a thickening agent made from a natural fermentation culture). The gum performs a similar function as gluten in baked goods.

Three recipes in the collection use sorghum flour and xanthan gum: *Sorghum Molasses Cookies* (page 200), *Sorghum Coconut-Oatmeal Cookies* (page 202), and *Sorghum Banana-Walnut Cookies* (page 204).

Another thickening agent used to add texture and structure in gluten-free baking is **arrowroot powder** (sometimes called arrowroot flour). It comes from a tropical American plant. The roots are processed to yield an edible starch similar to potato starch, corn starch or tapioca. Arrowroot powder is an important ingredient in *Gluten-Free Chocolate-Brownie Cookies* (page 194). For the best outcome, don't replace the powder with another starch.

Find arrowroot powder, sorghum flour and xanthan gum in health food stores.

LEAVENINGS

Baking powder and **baking soda** are used in many cookie recipes to improve and lighten texture. Both help dough expand and rise during baking. Double-acting baking powder is the kind used in this cookbook and is the type of most commercial powders. "Double-acting" means it gives a second push when the baking temperature reaches around 140 degrees F. This produces a taller and lighter cookie.

Baking powder and soda need to be fresh to perform well. Note expiration dates and replace them often. Important also, break up any lumps or clumps in powder or soda before measuring them. Leavenings have a bitter-metallic flavor that must be blended evenly into other ingredients. Read more about this on page XIV, COMBINING INGREDIENTS.

EGGS

I use large eggs throughout this book. All the recipes that call for eggs have been created, tested or simply made for as long as I can remember with large room-temperature eggs. I skip egg substitutes; they are 98 to 99% egg whites and lack the yolk-rich taste of whole eggs. When making cookies, I find the indulgence of full-fatty flavors well worth my time and effort— including honest-to-goodness eggs.

NUTS

A great many recipes include nuts, namely my favorites—pecans, walnuts, almonds, hazelnuts (filberts), cashews, macadamia nuts, and peanuts. Actually, peanuts are not a nut; they're a root legume but are used the same way as nuts. Since nuts (including peanuts) contain oil, they turn rancid over time unless refrigerated or frozen. I buy nuts in sealed bags from the grocery store and stow them away in the refrigerator as soon as I get home. Nuts have a high turnover in my fridge; rarely do I buy more nuts than I plan to use in a few weeks. Even if nuts are on sale, I make plans to quickly use them or sprinkle them generously over my morning cereal.

Toasted nuts are called for in several recipes. Toasting enhances their flavor and crisps them.

My method is to cook and stir nuts in a dry skillet on the stovetop until just fragrant (see Note page 17).

To finely grind nuts, use a food processor or an electric coffee grinder (see Note page 67).

CHOCOLATE

Semisweet, mint, bittersweet, unsweetened, and milk chocolate in the forms of chips and premium baking bars are used in the recipes. For example, **semisweet** chips—either mini or regular-size—work beautifully in *Chocolate-Chip Cookie Bars* (page 146). **Mint** chocolate chips are wonderful in *Chocolate Mint Cookies* (page 52), or substitute cream de menthe baking chips to produce a more sumptuous flavor. For recipes that call for dark chocolate such as *Chocolate-Dipped Coconut Macaroons* (page 156), buy a Ghirardelli **bittersweet 60% cacao** baking bar. When making *The Real Deal Chocolate Brownies* (page 134), you will need an **unsweetened 100% cacao** baking bar. Finally, **milk** chocolate is absolutely superb in *Pecan Turtle Triangles* (page 132)—use Ghirardelli milk chocolate chips.

Melted chocolate is used occasionally in the book to garnish cookies with a scant drizzle or decorative dip. Feel free to use it more often if you like. To melt chocolate, do so patiently in the microwave (see Note page 11). If you store chocolate in the refrigerator or freezer, do not unwrap it while allowing it to come to room temperature. Moisture will form on the surface of unwrapped cold or frozen chocolate, and this will—always—prevent it from melting smoothly. I learned this the hard way; spoiling lots of chocolate and not knowing why.

COCOA POWDER

I use **natural (non-alkalized) unsweetened cocoa powder**. Alkalized (Dutch-processed cocoa) is used in baking when the major leavening agent is baking powder. The cocoa is processed with alkali to neutralize its acidity. It has a mild flavor and is less acidic. Natural cocoa is used when the primary leavening agent is baking soda, as in virtually all the recipes using cocoa plus leavening in this book.

Natural cocoa is tangy-acidic with a strong chocolaty

flavor. In recipes that require no leavening, either powder may be used. Still, my choice is natural cocoa for its more assertive chocolate flavor.

ORANGE & LEMON ZEST

Several recipes call for the zest of an orange or lemon. It's important to mention how to properly remove and gather zest because just below the thin hued skin (the zest) lies the **bitter white pith**. Don't use a grater; it shreds the zest, digging deeply enough to reach the pith. Use a stainless steel microplane with razor-sharp teeth to gently shave the delicate skin. Lightly stroke the plane over the well washed surface of the fruit and collect the shavings. The zest will have the intense, tangy-citrus flavor of the fruit without a hint of bitter, guaranteed.

MEASURING INGREDIENTS

Using the right ingredients—plus measuring them correctly—will increase your odds of **consistently** producing good-tasting cookies. Accurate measurements are absolutely indispensable for cookies to turn out good the first time you make a recipe—and every time after that.

Be sure your kitchen is equipped with proper measuring spoons and cups. You need to have graduated spoons to measure small amounts of liquids such as extracts and dry ingredients like spices. Have on hand liquid measuring cups, a 1-cup measure that's also marked for smaller increments and a 2-cup measure for larger amounts. A set of graduated, nestled-measuring cups for dry ingredients like flour is a must.

Measure small amounts of dry ingredients with the exact size measuring spoon. Scoop the spoon into the ingredient and then level it at the rim with a straight-edge spatula. When measuring small amounts of liquid, use the exact size spoon. Pour the liquid just to the top without letting it spill over.

For larger amounts of liquid, place a measuring cup on a level surface and slowly pour the liquid in until it reaches the desired line. Don't lift the cup to read the measurement; always bend down and read it at eye level. Liquid is slightly concave because of surface tension, and it's the bottom "line" of the inward curve that should be even with the line on the cup.

Dry measuring cups are used for flours, sugars, cocoa powder, chopped nuts, flaked coconut, chocolate chips, cookie crumbs, cut up dried fruits and raisins, and dry cereals like oatmeal. A dry measuring cup is also used to measure ingredients such as pumpkin puree, sour cream, fruit preserves, apple sauce, and mashed bananas. These ingredients are not "dry," but they mound when measured. A dry measuring cup allows the ingredient to be leveled at the rim with accuracy.

Lightly spoon powdery ingredients like flour and powdered sugar into the cup and then level it at the rim. Never shake or tap the cup to compact an ingredient; just heap it in and level it. However, brown sugar needs to be pressed down and firmly packed. Brown sugar should hold the shape of the cup when it's turned out.

Buy butter in sticks that are wrapped in wax paper with markings for tablespoons, ¼ and ⅓ cups. Simply cut off the amount needed, or use the number of sticks called for in a recipe. Vegetable shortening also comes in convenient packaging that's already marked with accurate portions.

COMBINING INGREDIENTS

Among the recipes in this book, I give instructions for sifting the dry ingredients when I think it will improve a cookie. Otherwise, whisking is adequate—when done thoroughly and mindfully.

Sifting is important when baking powder and baking soda are included in the ingredients. Sifting eliminates lumps of soda and powder. Even tiny clumps of leavening can produce a bitter-metallic flavor pocket in baked goods. Taste a pinch of powder and soda to experience the flavor. It will re-mind you to always break up lumps before measuring the leavenings, especially if you choose to merely whisk the dry ingredients together.

When a recipe includes cocoa powder and/or a number of spices, I sift the dry ingredients and then briefly whisk the mixture. Try this the next time you sift flour with cocoa. You'll see, by contrast of color, how much more homogeneous the mixture becomes if followed by a brief whisking. This double-step assures me of a good distribution of all the dry components. I use a large, wire-mesh sieve instead of a traditional sifter because it's easy to fill and has a large capacity.

Softened butter is called for in many recipes. This requires the butter to be held at room temperature until it has a soft consistency, allowing it to be beaten with the sugar until light and fluffy. Beating incorporates air into the fat to give cookies better volume and a lighter texture. To achieve "light and fluffy," the butter and sugar must be beaten for several min-utes. Most recipes suggest a specific length of time for this, often between 3 to 7 minutes. The mixture will become lightened in color and texture.

When adding a flour mixture to buttery-moist ingredients, reduce the mixer speed to low and add the dry ingredients slowly. Better yet, use a wooden spoon or rubber spatula to gradually stir in the flour mixture just until incorporated into a dough. Beating too long and vigorously over develops gluten protein in the flour, resulting in hard-to-chew cookies that are more like DOG BISCUITS.

TECHNIQUES & TIPS

Beautiful homemade cookies are a realistic goal. A few simple techniques used with **regularity** will produce good-looking cookies every time. This requires just basic understandings and less skill than you may think. Nothing about this is too difficult.

HANDLING COOKIE DOUGH

When making DROP and MOLDED cookies, consistently use either a 1- or ½-tablespoon measure to portion the dough. This produces cookies of uniform size and ensures that the recipe yields and baking times are accurate. Use a butter knife to heap dough into the spoon, level it off and scoop it out. With the tip of the knife, give DROP cookies a pat or two to coax them into a nice shape.

When making MOLDED cookies, drop all the measured dough onto the baking sheets first and then go back and shape dough into balls, logs, crescents, flattened balls—whatever is called for. This "assembly-line" process streamlines the work and produces a beautifully consistent batch of cookies.

Cookie dough that seems too soft to handle will become

more manageable if chilled. For dough that warms quickly and becomes very soft, work with small portions and keep the rest cold until needed. When rolling cookie dough on a floured surface, you want to avoid using too much extra flour. Chilling the dough makes it manageable so less flour is needed. Too much flour results in coarse cookies.

To ensure light and tender ROLLED cookies, scraps of dough should be rolled no more than two times. Keep cut shapes all about the same size and thickness so they bake evenly and have consistent crispness. (The thinner the dough is rolled, the crisper the cookies.) Lift cut dough to the baking sheet with a thin-bladed, off-set spatula (pancake turner). The angle of this tool lets you get under the soft-cut dough more easily, so you can preserve the pristine shape of each cookie.

Slice-and-bake REFRIGERATOR cookie dough is wonderful to work with. Logs can be made in advance and stored in the freezer for up to two months. Little time is spent on shaping cookies; logs are simply cut crosswise into round slices. Very little time is spent thawing the dough since it slices best when very cold or still slightly frozen.

Many BAR & SQUARE recipes require the making of a bottom crust. Sometimes the crust mixture resembles fine crumbs that are easily pressed into a pan, but often it's a sticky dough. Manage stickiness by using floured or slightly moistened fingertips. A rubber spatula lightly coated with cooking spray can also help spread and press sticky dough from the center of the pan to the edges.

When making PRESSED cookies, be sure your baking sheets are at room temperature. Hold the press so that it rests on the sheet, and raise it when enough dough has been pressed to form your desired shape. If needed, wait a moment to allow dough to adhere to the sheet before lifting the press. The doughs for *Cocoa Spritz* (page 20), *Orange Ribbon Spritz* (page 22), and *Almond Spritz* (page 24) are all wonderful to work with. If your kitchen isn't overheated, the dough doesn't even need to be chilled before pressing. Chill the dough for about one hour if it becomes difficult to work with or the cookies don't hold their shape when baked.

BAKING SHEETS & PANS

Dark, non-stick sheets concentrate heat and often cause cookies to brown too quickly. Shiny-metal sheets reflect heat away from the cookies and typically produce light golden, evenly-baked crusts. Sometimes though, a particular cookie will actually brown best on a dark sheet. When a cookie is sensitive to over-browning or will do better on a dark sheet, I "Note" or mention it in the recipe. Otherwise, a good rule to follow is this: If using a dark sheet, check cookies at the shortest baking time given; if using a shiny sheet, you may have to bake cookies a minute or two longer.

The size of the baking pan is important when making BARS & SQUARES. Always use the pan size specified. The wrong pan changes baking time and texture. A pan that's too big results in a thin dried-out cookie slab; a too small pan produces a slab that's gummy and under-baked in the center.

When a greased baking sheet or pan is called for, you can use just a light application of either butter, shortening or cooking spray. Cookies that have a large percentage of fat can be baked on ungreased sheets. Bar cookies that require a greased pan turn out well when **heavy-duty non-stick aluminum foil** is used to line the pan (for details, see Note page 149).

It's important to line baking sheets with **parchment paper** when making chocolaty cookies and macaroons that can burn easily, cookies with sticky candied fruits, and meringues that have a large portion of egg white and typically stick to the pan. For sensitive cookies, I list parchment paper above the ingredient list of the recipe. Personally, I'm not a big fan of parchment paper unless it's necessary. Silicone bakeware is not my preference either. I love the toasted flavor of cookies baked on metal sheets, especially when nuts are in the dough.

BAKING COOKIES

Always preheat the oven, and have the rack positioned in the middle unless otherwise directed.

I prefer to bake sheets of cookies one-at-a-time. I place my sheet in the oven horizontally instead of vertically so cookies brown evenly without having to be rotated. Rarely, I'll bake two sheets together. If you bake two at a time, be sure the sheets don't touch and rotate them from front to back halfway through the baking time for even browning. Meringues are an exception. Since they bake at a low temperature and barely brown, meringues can be baked two sheets at a time without rotating.

STORING COOKIES

I freeze cookies—almost always—and especially during the busy holiday baking season which begins for me right after Halloween. I freeze butter cookies as soon as they cool to room temperature, at the peak of fresh-baked flavor. Cookies that are coated with jimmies, soft powdered sugar icing, or dipped into melted chocolate, need to be flash-frozen before stowing away. This prevents the soft coatings from becoming dented or misshaped. I put an entire rack of completely cooled cookies on a large jelly-roll pan and carefully slide it into the freezer for 15 to 20 minutes. This thoroughly firms the surface. Then I quickly stack cookies between layers of saran in airtight-plastic containers. I use a strip of masking tape to label containers, writing the date, cookie type and number of cookies on the strip. I stick the tape on the container before freezing; it won't stick if you wait until the plastic becomes cold.

I store each cookie type separately, and only mix frozen

cookies in one container toward the end of the holidays when the numbers dwindle down. It's a joy to dip into this finale container on New Year's Eve to partake of what's left—and the cookies are still fresh and beautiful.

Even when it's not the holidays, I store most cookies in the freezer. They last longer, are fresher when I want them, and stay out of sight and mind for at least awhile. In the interest of freshness, I try not to hold cookies longer than two months. They won't spoil in the freezer, but cookies begin to change in flavor and texture with prolonged freezing. I thaw cookies naked from the container at room temperature. It's so easy. Simply place the number of cookies desired on a plate and let them sit on the counter top for 10 to 20 minutes.

If you choose to not freeze cookies, store them in a moisture-proof container with a tight-fitting lid or a zipper-top plastic bag. Hold them at a cool room temperature away from heat and sunlight.

Always store crisp and soft cookies separately.

Most BARS & SQUARES can be stored in the pan covered with foil or saran and held at a cool room temperature for a day or two. An exception is *No-Bake Peanut Butter Oat Squares* (page 210).

These soft squares should be stored in the freezer, and are actually best when eaten frozen. *My Favorite Granola Bars* (page 212) freeze well for longer storage, too. A few squares, such as *Pumpkin Pie Squares* (page 110) and *Strawberry Cheesecake Squares* (page 114), are perishable and need to be stored in the refrigerator and served chilled. When special attention is needed for storage, it's mentioned either in the text above the recipe or a "Note" at the bottom of the page.

Lastly, let your own common sense and creativity guide as you focus on the process of making cookies. Keeping distractions to a minimum is my personal way of entering fully into the experience of working with a recipe and the ingredients. Furthermore, I find multitasking counterproductive; it removes me from the step-by-step process of creating something truly special. A focused mind has always produced my best outcomes. Maybe this will be helpful for you, too.

HOLIDAY COLLECTION

Chilly Chicago weather and the approach of winter holidays herald—for me—a busy cookie-baking season. Over the years, my collection of holiday recipes grew from the favorable responses from family, friends and neighbors. Their enthusiastic feedback inspired me to gather the recipes below—for you. Enjoy!

MY HUSBAND'S FAVORITE BUTTER COOKIES

When I married Jeff, Mom gave me the newest (1972) Betty Crocker's Cookbook. The Marzipan cookie recipe intrigued me. I decreased the flour by one-half cup and used the dough to make cut-out cookies. I've made these cookies every holiday since. They are my husband's favorite; he likes them in the shape of Christmas trees adorned with rainbow sprinkles.

Many, many people love these cookies!

- Makes about 4 dozen -

INGREDIENTS

	Rainbow sprinkles, red and green sugars, chocolate jimmies, etc.
1	cup (2 sticks) unsalted butter, softened
½	cup granulated sugar
1	teaspoon pure almond extract
2	cups all-purpose flour

DIRECTIONS

In a large bowl and with a mixer on medium speed, cream the butter until smooth, about 30 seconds. Gradually add the sugar and then beat until very light and fluffy, 5 to 7 minutes. Beat in the extract. Reduce speed to low. Add the flour in 4 parts, mixing just until each addition is incorporated. Shape the dough into a square; wrap in saran and refrigerate overnight. The dough will be perfect to work with.

Next day, keeping the dough wrapped, allow it to return to a cool room temperature.

Preheat the oven to 325 degrees F.

Slice the dough into 4 portions; work with one portion at a time. On a lightly floured surface, roll the dough to a scant ¼-inch thickness. Cut into shapes. Use a thin bladed, off-set spatula (pancake turner) to transfer cookies to ungreased baking sheets, spacing about 1 inch apart. Decorate with sprinkles, sugars, jimmies, whatever you like.

Bake for about 12 to 15 minutes or until just slightly browned around the edges. Transfer cookies to a wire rack when firm enough to move; cool completely.

Note: For delicate browning, use only shiny-metal baking sheets.

FRUIT & NUT COOKIES

This recipe lived for decades on a scrap of paper tucked inside Mom's 1940's cookbook. Originally, it called for roasted Brazil nuts—delicious! However, roasting and rolling off the skins is a lot of work, so I substitute a combo of toasted almonds and walnuts. I also resized the recipe; you can double it.

- Makes about 4 dozen –

INGREDIENTS

	Parchment paper
¾	cup slivered almonds, toasted
¾	cup shelled walnuts, toasted and then coarsely chopped
1¼	cups all-purpose flour
½	teaspoon ground cinnamon
½	teaspoon baking soda
½	teaspoon salt
4	ounces candied cherries, quartered (about ¾ cup)
4	ounces candied pineapple, chopped (about ¾ cup)
½	cup chopped dates
½	cup unsalted butter (1 stick), softened
¾	cup granulated sugar
1	large egg

DIRECTIONS

Toast the nuts separately in a clean skillet (see Note page 17). Set aside and cool to room temperature.

Line baking sheets with parchment paper. Set aside.

Preheat the oven to 400 degrees F.

Into a 1-quart bowl, sift together the flour, cinnamon, baking soda, and salt; whisk briefly. Set aside.

In a medium bowl, stir and toss together the cherries, pineapple, and dates. Add the toasted nuts and continue to stir the mixture until well combined. Set aside.

In a large bowl and with a mixer on medium speed, cream the butter. Gradually add the sugar; beat until very well blended. Beat in the egg. Reduce speed to low. Add the flour mixture in 3 parts. Stir in the fruit and nuts. Drop the dough by level tablespoons onto the prepared baking sheets, spacing about 2 inches apart.

Bake for 8 minutes or until just lightly golden. Cool cookies on the sheet for 2 to 3 minutes. Transfer to a wire rack; cool completely.

VIENNESE ALMOND CRESCENTS

I've made these crescents for over 40 years. I chop natural sliced almonds because they have their skins intact. This produces cookies with brown flecks, adding overall appeal. Plus, the tiny angles of the nuts subtly enhance texture. The cookies bake best on dark, non-stick sheets; the bottoms become toasty and without a hint of bitter-burnt flavor.

- Makes about 4 dozen -

INGREDIENTS

	Extra powdered sugar to coat cookies (about 1 cup)
1	cup (2 sticks) unsalted butter, softened
6	tablespoons powdered sugar
2	cups all-purpose flour
2	cups finely chopped natural sliced almonds

DIRECTIONS

Preheat the oven to 350 degrees F.

In a large bowl and with a mixer on medium speed, cream the butter until smooth, about 30 seconds. Add 6 tablespoons powdered sugar and continue to beat until very light and fluffy, 4 to 5 minutes.

Reduce speed to low. Gradually mix in the flour. Stir in the nuts with a wooden spoon.

Use 1 level tablespoon of dough per cookie and shape into logs, bending slightly midway to form the crescent shape. Place crescents on ungreased baking sheets, spacing about 1½ inches apart.

Bake for 20 minutes or until lightly golden around the edges and golden brown on the bottoms. Meanwhile, put the extra powdered sugar into a shallow bowl.

While still quite hot, quickly roll each crescent in powdered sugar to coat the tops and sides—leave the bottoms naked. The sugar will melt on the hot surface. Place the crescents on a wire rack and cool completely. Store in the freezer (see Note below).

> **Note:** TO FIRM THE MELTED POWDERED-SUGAR COATING, flash-freeze the crescents. After thoroughly cooling, put the wire rack of cookies on a large jelly-roll pan and place the whole thing into the freezer for about 20 minutes. Then quickly stack the cookies between layers of saran in a sturdy container and stow in the freezer. When it's time to serve, simply take out the number of crescents you wish to use and arrange them on a tray. The cookies will defrost quickly and retain their lovely sweet coating unscathed.

PECAN LOGS

This cookie has the most excellent flavor of pecans, butter, chocolate and vanilla. Skip shiny-metal baking sheets or parchment paper and bake the cookies directly on a dark, non-stick sheet. They will brown perfectly and have a buttery-toasted flavor. Dark sheets often brown cookies too fast and too much, but not in this case.

- Makes about 4 dozen –

INGREDIENTS

	Wax paper
1	cup unsalted butter (2 sticks), softened
½	cup powdered sugar
1	teaspoon pure vanilla extract
½	teaspoon salt
1½	cups all-purpose flour—plus 2 tablespoons
2	cups chopped pecans
	About 1 cup semisweet chocolate chips, melted (see Note below)

DIRECTIONS

Preheat the oven to 325 degrees F.

In a large bowl and with a mixer on medium speed, cream the butter until smooth, about 30 seconds. Slowly add the powdered sugar; beat until light and fluffy, 4 to 5 minutes. Beat in the extract and salt. Reduce speed to low. Mix in the flour in about 4 parts. Stir in the nuts with a wooden spoon.

Use 1 level tablespoon of dough per cookie and shape into logs. Space about 2 inches apart on ungreased baking sheets.

Bake for 20 minutes or until browned around the edges and on the bottoms. Transfer cookies to a wire rack when firm enough to move; cool completely.

Dip just the tip of each log into melted chocolate and then place on a large wax-paper-lined, jelly-roll pan. Put the pan into the freezer for about 15 minutes to firm the chocolate.

> **Note:** TO MELT CHOCOLATE, put it into a microwave-safe bowl and microwave on HIGH, stopping to stir every 15 to 20 seconds. Repeat until almost melted (some pieces should be visible); stir until smooth.

> **Note:** Store the cookies frozen in an airtight container between layers of saran.

COCOA SNOWBALLS

The original recipe didn't include chocolate jimmies—they're my contri-bution. Finished cookies were simply dusted with powdered sugar. Use either chopped walnuts or pecans. Sometimes, I use a combo of nuts—whatever is at hand. The cookies are always great, and the dough is wonderful to work with.

- Makes about 5 dozen -

INGREDIENTS

	Parchment paper
	About 1½ cups chocolate jimmies
2	cups all-purpose flour
½	cup natural (non-alkalized) unsweetened cocoa powder
⅛	teaspoon salt
1¼	cups unsalted butter (2½ sticks), softened
⅔	cup granulated sugar
2	teaspoons pure vanilla extract
2	cups finely chopped nuts (walnuts are my first choice)

DIRECTIONS

Preheat the oven to 350 degrees F.

Line baking sheets with parchment paper. Set aside.

Into a medium bowl, sift the flour with the cocoa powder and salt; whisk briefly. Set aside.

In a large bowl and with a mixer on medium speed, cream the butter for 30 seconds. Gradually add the sugar and then beat until very light and fluffy, 5 to 7 minutes. Beat in the extract. Reduce speed to low. Add the flour mixture in 4 parts. Stir in the nuts with a wooden spoon.

Put the jimmies into a shallow bowl. Use 1 level tablespoon of dough per cookie and shape into balls. Roll each ball in jimmies to coat the top and sides—leave the bottoms naked. Space about 2 inches apart on the prepared baking sheets.

Bake for 20 minutes or until just baked through. Do not allow to brown. Cool cookies on the sheet for several minutes before transferring to a wire rack (see Note below).

Note: THE JIMMIES WILL BE SOFT!!! Use a thin-bladed, off-set spatula (pancake turner) to carefully transfer cookies off the baking sheet and onto a rack; cool completely. Place the rack on a jelly-roll pan and put the whole thing into the freezer for about 15 minutes to thoroughly firm the jimmies. Then stack cookies between layers of saran in a sturdy container and store in the freezer. When thawed, the cookies will be perfectly beautiful.

COCOA CONFETTI COOKIES

These good-looking, dark chocolate cookies are soft, chewy and very delicious. Below, I use one level tablespoon of dough per cookie, but you can use one-half tablespoon for smaller cookies. It will double the yield; just watch the baking time closely.

- Makes about 34 cookies -

INGREDIENTS

	Extra butter to grease the baking sheets
	About 1 cup rainbow jimmies
1⅔	cups all-purpose flour
½	cup natural (non-alkalized) unsweetened cocoa powder
½	teaspoon baking soda
¼	teaspoon salt
½	cup (1 stick) unsalted butter, softened
½	cup granulated sugar
½	cup firmly packed light-brown sugar
1	large egg
1	teaspoon pure vanilla extract

DIRECTIONS

Preheat the oven to 350 degrees F.

Lightly grease baking sheets. Set aside.

Into a medium bowl, sift together the flour, cocoa, baking soda, and salt; whisk briefly. Set aside.

In a large bowl and with a mixer on medium speed, cream the butter for 30 seconds. Gradually add both sugars; beat until well blended, about 2 minutes. Beat in the egg and extract. Reduce speed to low.

Gradually beat in as much flour mixture as you can; use a wooden spoon to blend in remaining flour.

Put rainbow jimmies into a shallow bowl. Use 1 level tablespoon of dough per cookie and shape into balls. Roll each ball in jimmies to coat allover. Space about 2 inches apart on the prepared baking sheets. Use the bottom of a drinking glass to flatten balls into a ⅜- to ½-inch thickness.

Bake for 8 to 10 minutes or just until set. Cool cookies on the sheet until firm enough to move, 3 to 4 minutes. Transfer to a wire rack and cool completely (see Note page 13).

TOASTED TRIPLE-NUT SNOWBALLS

Round-up leftover nuts from holiday baking and make these cookies for the New Year. Toasting the nuts enhances their overall flavor and crisps them. Use either almond or vanilla extract or a combo of each to equal one teaspoon, as you like.

- Makes about 4 dozen –

INGREDIENTS

	Extra powdered sugar to coat and dust cookies (about 1 cup)
⅓	cup sliced almonds
⅓	cup chopped pecans
⅓	cup chopped walnuts
1¼	cups (2½ sticks) unsalted butter, softened
½	cup powdered sugar
1	large egg
1	teaspoon pure almond or vanilla extract
2¼	cups all-purpose flour

DIRECTIONS

Toast each nut type separately in a clean skillet (see Note below). Set aside; cool to room temperature.

Preheat the oven to 350 degrees F.

In a large bowl and with a mixer on medium speed, cream the butter until smooth, about 30 seconds. Gradually add ½ cup powdered sugar; beat until light and fluffy, 4 to 5 minutes. Beat in the egg and extract. Use a wooden spoon to gradually stir in the flour just until combined. Stir in the toasted nuts.

Use 1 level tablespoon of dough per cookie and shape into balls. Space about 2 inches apart on ungreased baking sheets.

Bake for 13 to 15 minutes or until browned on the bottoms. Meanwhile, put the extra powdered sugar into a shallow bowl.

Roll warm cookies in the extra powdered sugar to coat allover; place on a rack and cool completely. Dust with additional powdered sugar dredged through a fine-mesh sieve.

> **Note:** TO TOAST NUTS such as sliced or slivered almonds, pecans, and walnuts, place them in a dry skillet on the stovetop over medium heat and cook and stir just until fragrant. Immediately transfer to a plate to cool. If left in the skillet, the nuts will continue to cook and become burnt and bitter.

CINNAMON SNOWBALLS

Cake flour and crushed cornflakes produce an interesting, tender texture. This is a nice dough to work with. Balls may be flattened with fork tines or molded into shapes. Add variation by dusting some cookies with powdered sugar and others with cinnamon sugar.

- Makes about 3½ dozen –

INGREDIENTS

	Powdered sugar for dusting (about 2 tablespoons)
2	cups cake flour
½	cup finely crushed cornflakes (about 2 cups whole flakes—see Note below)
1	teaspoon ground cinnamon
1	cup (2 sticks) unsalted butter, softened
⅓	cup granulated sugar
2	teaspoons pure vanilla extract
1	cup chopped nuts (my preference is walnuts)

DIRECTIONS

Preheat the oven to 350 degrees F.

In a medium bowl, whisk the cake flour with the cornflakes and cinnamon. Set aside.

In a large bowl and with a mixer on medium speed, cream the butter until smooth, about 30 seconds. Slowly add the granulated sugar and then beat until light and fluffy, 4 to 5 minutes. Beat in the extract. Use a wooden spoon to gradually stir in the flour mixture. Stir in the nuts.

Use 1 level tablespoon of dough per cookie and shape into balls. Space about 2 inches apart on ungreased baking sheets.

Bake for 20 minutes or until firm and golden brown. Remove to a wire rack. Dust hot cookies with either powdered sugar dredged through a fine-mesh sieve or Cinnamon Sugar For Dusting (see Note below). Cool the cookies and then dust again if desired.

> **Note:** TO FINELY CRUSH CORNFLAKES, and to also make graham cracker or cookie crumbs and to crush peppermint candies, put them into a sturdy, zipper-top plastic bag and crush with a rolling pin or wooden mallet.

> **Note:** CINNAMON SUGAR FOR DUSTING: Mix 1 tablespoon granulated sugar with ½ teaspoon ground cinnamon.

COCOA SPRITZ (and more)

You can mold this extraordinary cookie dough into all sorts of shapes (balls, crescents, logs, balls flattened with fork tines, or pressed cookies—spritz). I use a cookie press with the flower-plate tip to make Christmas wreaths. This dough truly lends itself to creativity—feel free to do with it as you like.

- Makes about 4 dozen -

INGREDIENTS

Decorative cookie sprinkles

1½   cups all-purpose flour

¼   cup natural (non-alkalized) unsweetened cocoa powder

¾   cup (1½ sticks) unsalted butter, softened

½   cup granulated sugar

1   egg yolk from a large egg

1   teaspoon pure almond or vanilla extract

DIRECTIONS

Into a medium bowl, sift the flour with the cocoa powder; whisk briefly. Set aside.

In a large bowl and with a mixer on medium speed, cream the butter until smooth. Gradually add the sugar; beat for 3 to 4 minutes. Beat in the egg yolk and extract. Reduce speed to low. Gradually add the flour mixture, beating in as much as you can with the mixer. Stir in remaining flour with a wooden spoon. Cover the bowl with saran and chill until the dough is just slightly stiff and not at all hard, about 30 minutes. (If your kitchen isn't particularly overheated, you may not need to chill the dough.)

Preheat the oven to 375 degrees F.

Fill a cookie press fitted with the flower-plate tip or another tip shape— whatever you like. Press out cookies onto ungreased baking sheets, spacing about 2 inches apart. Sprinkle with decorative sugars.

Bake for 7 to 9 minutes or until set. Remove the sheet to a wire rack and allow cookies to stand just until firm enough to move, 1 to 2 minutes. Transfer cookies to a wire rack and cool completely.

ORANGE RIBBON SPRITZ

Here's a crisp-tender cookie with an unusual shape, texture and tangy orange flavor. It looks great among other cookies on my holiday trays, offering an intriguing variation in form and flavor.

- Makes about 5 Dozen –

INGREDIENTS

1	cup (2 sticks) unsalted butter, softened
1	cup powdered sugar
¼	teaspoon salt
1	large egg
½	teaspoon pure vanilla extract
	Shaved zest from 2 large navel oranges*
2⅓	cups all-purpose flour

DIRECTIONS

In a large bowl and with a mixer on medium speed, cream the butter until smooth, about 30 seconds. Gradually add 1 cup powdered sugar; add the salt and continue to beat until very fluffy, 4 to 5 minutes. Beat in the egg, extract, and zest. Reduce speed to low. Add the flour in 4 parts, beating in as much as you can with the mixer. Stir in any remaining flour with a wooden spoon. Cover the bowl with saran and chill until the dough is slightly stiff but not hard, about 30 minutes.

Preheat the oven to 400 degrees F.

Fill a cookie press fitted with the bar-plate tip. Press dough in strips, about 1 inch apart, down the length of ungreased baking sheets. Cut the strips into 2½-inch pieces; leave the pieces in place.

Bake for 5 to 7 minutes or until lightly browned on the edges. Transfer cookies to a wire rack to cool. If desired, use a pastry brush to lightly coat the cookies with Orange Glaze (below); allow to dry.

ORANGE GLAZE (OPTIONAL)

INGREDIENTS

½	cup powdered sugar
2	tablespoons orange juice

DIRECTIONS

Simply mix the sugar with the juice in a small bowl.

*See **Orange & Lemon Zest** (page XIII).

ALMOND SPRITZ

As an option, almond flour can replace the work of finely grinding almonds. The substitution in this decades-old recipe works beautifully. Almond flour streamlines the effort and produces a dough that's perfect to work with. For another recipe that uses almond flour—instead of grinding the hard nuts—see **Chinese New Year Nut Balls** *(page 104).*

- Makes about 4½ dozen -

INGREDIENTS

	Decorative sugars
1¾	cups all-purpose flour
¼	cup finely ground almonds* (or substitute ¼ cup raw almond flour)
½	teaspoon salt
¾	cup (1½ sticks) unsalted butter, softened
¾	cup granulated sugar
1	large egg
½	teaspoon pure almond extract

DIRECTIONS

In a medium bowl, whisk together the all-purpose flour, ground almonds (or almond flour) and salt. Set aside.

In a large bowl and with a mixer on medium speed, cream the butter for 30 seconds. Gradually add the sugar; beat for 3 minutes. Beat in the egg and extract. Reduce speed to low. Slowly add the flour mixture, beating in as much as you can with the mixer. Stir in remaining flour with a wooden spoon. Cover the bowl and refrigerate until the dough is just slightly stiff but not hard, about 30 minutes.

Preheat the oven to 350 degrees F.

Fill a cookie press fitted with the plate tip of your choice. Press out cookies onto ungreased baking sheets, spacing about 2 inches apart. Sprinkle with decorative sugars, as you like.

Bake for 10 to 12 minutes or until lightly browned around the edges. Transfer cookies to a wire rack and cool completely.

* See Note page 67

NEAPOLITAN
REFRIGERATOR COOKIES

Three layers of flavor—orange, chocolate and pecan—combine in this cleverly molded slice-and-bake recipe. For another use of the basic dough, consider **Sunset Refrigerator Cookies** *(page 28).*

- Makes about 4 dozen –

INGREDIENTS

Wax paper and aluminum foil

BASIC DOUGH

2½   cups all-purpose flour

½   teaspoon baking powder

½   teaspoon salt

1   cup (2 sticks) unsalted butter, softened

⅔   cup granulated sugar

2   egg yolks from 2 large eggs

1   teaspoon pure vanilla extract

FLAVOR LAYERS

2   teaspoons shaved orange zest*

1   ounce bittersweet chocolate, melted and cooled to room temperature

¼   cup finely chopped pecans

DIRECTIONS

Into a medium bowl, sift together the flour, baking powder, and salt; whisk briefly. Set aside.

In a large bowl and with a mixer on medium speed, cream the butter for 30 seconds. Gradually add the sugar; beat for 3 minutes. Beat in the egg yolks and extract. Reduce speed to low. Slowly add the flour mixture, beating in as much as you can with the mixer. Stir in remaining flour with a wooden spoon.

Divide dough into 3 equal parts; place in 3 different bowls. (If you have a kitchen scale, divide dough into three 8-ounce portions.) Work zest into 1 part, chocolate into 1 part, and nuts into 1 part.

Line the bottom and sides of a 9x5-inch loaf pan with wax paper. (Be sure the paper extends up to the top of the pan.) Spread orange dough on the bottom. Press chocolate dough over the orange; press nut dough over chocolate. Tightly cover the pan with foil and refrigerate overnight.

Next day, preheat the oven to 350 degrees F.

Uncover the pan. Remove dough by lifting the wax paper edges; place it on a cutting surface. Cut the slab in half, lengthwise. Cut each half crosswise into ¼-inch slices. Place on ungreased baking sheets, spacing about 1½ inches apart.

Bake for 15 minutes or until just lightly browned. Promptly transfer cookies to a wire rack when firm enough to move. (If left on the sheet too long, the cookies will stick.) Cool completely.

*See **Orange & Lemon Zest** (page XIII).

SUNSET REFRIGERATOR COOKIES

The same dough used to make **Neapolitan Refrigerator Cookies** *(page 26) is used to make these round slice-and-bake cookies. Egg yolks give the dough a rich golden hue, and red sugar crystals around the edges create the appearance of a sunset. However, feel free to use any colorful sugar—as you like.*

- Makes about 5 Dozen -

INGREDIENTS

Wax paper and saran

About ½ cup red sugar crystals

Parchment paper

1   batch BASIC DOUGH (page 26)

DIRECTIONS

Prepare BASIC DOUGH.

Divide the dough into two halves. (If you have a kitchen scale, each half will weigh about 12 ounces.) On a wax-paper surface, roll the halves into two logs approximately 10 inches long and 1½ inches in diameter.

Put the sugar crystals into a jelly-roll pan with a high rim; spread evenly. Roll logs in the sugar to coat. Tightly wrap each log separately in saran and refrigerate overnight.

Next day, preheat the oven to 350 degrees F.

Line baking sheets with parchment paper.

Unwrap the logs. Cut into ¼-inch-thick slices and place on the prepared baking sheets, spacing about 1½ inches apart.

Bake for about 15 minutes or until slightly browned. Transfer to a wire rack and cool completely.

SPICEY BUTTER COOKIES

This dough molds beautifully into thinly flattened cookies. Plus, it produces a cookie that doesn't spread a lot when baking, so it's perfect for sharply defined cut-out cookies, too. Similar recipes use molasses, resulting in a heavy-pungent aroma and flavor. These cookies are crisp, light and buttery.

- Makes about 7 dozen –

INGREDIENTS

	Parchment paper	⅛	teaspoon ground cloves
	Granulated sugar to flatten cookies (about ¼ cup)	1	cup (2 sticks) unsalted butter, softened
	Melted dark chocolate for garnish (optional)	1	cup firmly packed light-brown sugar
2½	cups all-purpose flour	½	teaspoon salt
¾	teaspoon ground cinnamon	1	egg yolk from a large egg
½	teaspoon ground ginger	1	large egg
¼	teaspoon ground nutmeg	2	teaspoons pure vanilla extract
¼	teaspoon ground allspice		

DIRECTIONS

Into a medium bowl, sift the flour with the next 5 ingredients (through cloves); whisk briefly. Set aside.

In a large bowl and with a mixer on medium speed, cream the butter for 30 seconds. Gradually add the brown sugar; beat until lightened and fluffy, 4 to 5 minutes. Beat in the salt and egg yolk; beat in the egg and extract. Reduce speed to low. Gradually beat in the flour mixture. Cover the bowl with saran and refrigerate for 1 hour.

Preheat the oven to 375 degrees F.

Line baking sheets with parchment paper. Put the granulated sugar into a small bowl.

Use 1 level tablespoon of dough per cookie and shape into balls. Place 2 inches apart on the prepared baking sheets. Flatten to a ⅛-inch thickness with the greased bottom of a drinking glass dipped into the granulated sugar. Alternatively, roll dough out on a lightly flowered surface and cut into shapes.

Bake for 6 to 8 minutes or until lightly browned. Immediately remove cookies from the sheet and place on a wire rack to cool. If desired, garnish cookies with just a scant drizzle of melted dark chocolate.

> **Note:** Store a day or two in a covered container at room temperature to let the flavors mellow. Freeze for longer storage.

FESTIVE OAT & COCONUT TARTLETS

Sweetened with brown sugar and honey, these wholesome oatmeal tarts are holiday perfect when topped with red-candied cherry halves. Top some with walnut halves to present a visual variety.

If you like, use green-candied cherries, too.

My husband loves these, though he's not a big fan of oatmeal cookies.

- Makes about 2 dozen -

INGREDIENTS

	Extra butter to grease the mini-muffin pan
	Candied cherries and walnut halves for garnish
1½	cups dry quick-cooking rolled oats (not instant or old-fashioned)
½	cup sweetened flaked coconut
½	cup chopped walnuts
½	cup all-purpose flour
½	cup (1 stick) unsalted butter
¾	cup firmly packed light-brown sugar
2	tablespoons honey

DIRECTIONS

Preheat the oven to 350 degrees F.

Grease 24 wells of a 1¾-inch mini-muffin pan. Set aside.

In a large bowl, mix together the first 4 ingredients (oats through flour). Set aside.

Put the butter, brown sugar, and honey into a 1½- or 2-quart saucepan and place over medium-low heat. Stirring frequently, bring the mixture to boiling. Pour over the dry ingredients; stir until well combined.

For each tartlet, gently press 1 level tablespoon of mixture into each well of the prepared muffin-pan tin. (Lightly moisten your finger tips to make this easy.) Top each tartlet with either a candied cherry half or walnut half.

Bake for 15 to 20 minutes. Cool for 10 minutes in the pan before removing. (Do not let tartlets remain in the pan; they can stick if cooled too long.) Run a thin knife blade around the edges to loosen.

Transfer to a wire rack and cool completely.

INDIVIDUAL FRUITCAKES

This recipe is wonderful; it presents the traditional fruitcake in a novel way. Plus, as the batter comes together, the fruity-boozy aroma will delight your senses. Sprinkle extra liquor over the cooled cakes if you like. Store them in an airtight container and hold at a cool room temperature.

- Makes 30 petite fruitcakes –

INGREDIENTS

- 30 2-inch mini-foil baking cups
     Candied cherries cut into
     halves and pecan or walnut
     halves for garnish
- 1   cup currants
- ⅓   cup brandy
- 1   cup all-purpose flour
- 1   teaspoon ground allspice
- ½   teaspoon ground cinnamon
- ¼   teaspoon salt
- ½   cup (1 stick) unsalted butter,
     softened
- ¼   cup firmly packed light-
     brown sugar
- 2   large eggs
- ¼   cup seedless black-raspberry
     preserves
     Shaved zest from 2 large
     navel oranges*
- 1   cup extra fancy fruitcake mix
     (diced mixed candied fruits)
- 1   cup coarsely chopped pecans
     or walnuts

DIRECTIONS

Soak the currants in ⅓ cup brandy overnight. Next day, drain off the liquid.
Set aside.

Preheat the oven to 325 degrees F.

Place mini-foil cups into 30 standard-size muffin pan cups. Set aside.

In a 1-quart bowl, thoroughly whisk together the flour, allspice, cinnamon,
and salt. Set aside.

In a large bowl and with a mixer on medium speed, cream the butter. Add
the brown sugar; beat until blended. Beat in the eggs one at a time and
then beat at high speed for 3 minutes. Beat in the preserves and zest. Use
a rubber spatula to stir in the flour mixture. Fold in currants, fruits, and
chopped nuts.

Spoon 1 heaping tablespoon of batter into each mini-foil cup. Top with a
walnut, pecan, or cherry half. Bake for 20 minutes. Transfer fruitcakes to
a wire rack and cool completely.

*See **Orange & Lemon Zest** (page XIII).

BRANDY JUMBLES

Inspired by a colonial "biscuit" recipe, these cookies represent a bit of Yankee heritage. The cookies are delicious when made very simply— with dark raisins—but nuts may be substituted, or use a combo of raisins and nuts to equal one cup. If desired, replace the liquor with milk.

- Makes about 4 dozen -

INGREDIENTS

2	cups all-purpose flour
1	teaspoon ground cinnamon
1	cup (2 sticks) unsalted butter, softened
1	cup granulated sugar
1	large egg
2	tablespoons brandy
½	teaspoon pure vanilla extract
1	cup raisins

DIRECTIONS

Preheat the oven to 375 degrees F.

In a medium bowl, thoroughly whisk together the flour and cinnamon. Set aside.

In a large bowl and with a mixer on medium speed, cream the butter for 30 seconds. Gradually add the sugar and then beat until very light and fluffy, 4 to 5 minutes. Beat in the egg, brandy, and extract. Use a wooden spoon to gradually stir in the flour mixture, stirring just until each addition is incorporated.

Stir in the raisins.

Drop level tablespoons of dough onto ungreased baking sheets, spacing about 2 inches apart.

Bake for 10 minutes or until golden brown around the edges. Transfer cookies to a wire rack as soon as they are firm enough to move. Cool completely.

BRANDY BALLS

Here's a no-bake confection that can be made with rum, bourbon, or— my favorite—brandy. Just be sure to use the liquor and not an extract. Use pecans or walnuts; pecans pair well with bourbon. To offer variety, coat some balls with powdered sugar and others with a mixture of cocoa and powdered sugar.

- Makes about 3 dozen –

INGREDIENTS

	Wax paper
1	cup powdered sugar
2	tablespoons natural (non-alkalized) unsweetened cocoa powder
2½	cups finely crushed vanilla wafers cookies (part of an 11 ounce package—see Note page 19)
1	cup chopped walnuts
¼	cup brandy
2	tablespoons light corn syrup

DIRECTIONS

Into a large bowl, sift 1 cup powdered sugar with 2 tablespoons cocoa powder. Thoroughly stir in the crushed cookies and nuts. Measure the brandy in a 1 cup measure; add the corn syrup and whisk together. Pour the mixture over the dry ingredients. Stir with a wooden spoon until well blended.

Shape level tablespoons of the mixture into balls and place on a wax-paper-lined jelly-roll pan. Then roll each ball in either powdered sugar or Cocoa Sugar (below) to coat allover. Let the balls stand uncovered overnight. Next day, layer between sheets of wax paper in an airtight container.

COCOA SUGAR

INGREDIENTS

¼	cup powdered sugar
2	tablespoons natural (non-alkalized) unsweetened cocoa powder

DIRECTIONS

Into a small bowl—and using a small fine-mesh sieve—sift the powdered sugar with the cocoa powder. Then whisk the mixture to thoroughly blend it.

Note: Store Brandy Balls for up to 3 weeks in the fridge or freezer; the overall flavor mellows and gets even better over time.

RUM-ESPRESSO COOKIES

A lovely feature of this cookie is the encrusted pecans on the bottom and outer edges. Underside nuts become lightly toasted as the cookies bake, and the overall-combined flavor of rum, espresso and toasted pecans is fabulous.

- Makes about 3½ dozen -

INGREDIENTS

	Extra butter to grease the baking sheets
	About 1½ cups chopped pecans
1	teaspoon instant espresso power
1	tablespoon boiling water
1½	cups all-purpose flour
1½	teaspoons baking powder
¼	teaspoon salt
½	cup (1 stick) unsalted butter, softened
1	cup firmly packed light-brown sugar
2	large eggs
½	teaspoon rum extract

DIRECTIONS

In a small cup or bowl, dissolve the espresso powder in boiling water. Set aside to cool.

Into a medium bowl, sift together the flour, baking powder, and salt; whisk briefly. Set aside.

In a large bowl and with a mixer on medium speed, cream the butter. Gradually add the brown sugar; beat until well combined. Add the eggs one at a time; beat in the extract and espresso. Use a wooden spoon to stir in the flour mixture in 4 parts. Cover the bowl with saran and refrigerate overnight.

Next day, preheat the oven to 350 degrees F.

Lightly grease baking sheets. Set aside.

Put nuts into a shallow bowl. Use 1 level tablespoon of dough per cookie and shape into balls. (This is a sticky dough; lightly coat your palms with cooking spray if needed.) Roll balls in nuts to coat allover; place on the prepared baking sheets, spacing about 2 inches apart.

Bake for about 10 minutes or until nicely browned. Transfer the cookies to a wire rack when they are firm enough to move. Cool completely.

PEPPERMINT STARS

I make small stars and use them to dot my holiday cookie trays. Scattered over an assortment of offerings, the festive gems invite people to nibble. Little stars look good in a candy dish, too.

- Makes about 6 dozen 1-inch or 3 dozen 2-inch cookies –

INGREDIENTS

	About 10 starlight peppermint candies, crushed (see Note page 19)
1⅓	cups all-purpose flour
1	teaspoon baking powder
⅓	cup unsalted butter, softened
¼	cup granulated sugar
1	large egg
¼	teaspoon pure peppermint extract

DIRECTIONS

Into a medium bowl, sift together the flour and baking powder; whisk briefly. Set aside.

In a large bowl and with a mixer on medium speed, cream the butter. Gradually add the sugar; beat for 2 to 3 minutes. Beat in the egg and extract. Reduce speed to low. Add the flour mixture in 4 parts.

Gather the dough and shape it into a square; wrap in saran and refrigerate for 1 hour.

Preheat the oven to 375 degrees F.

Divide dough into 4 portions; work with one portion at a time. On a floured surface, roll to a ¼-inch thickness. Cut with either a 1- or 2-inch star shaped cutter. Place on ungreased baking sheets, spacing about 1½ inches apart.

Bake 1-inch cookies for about 6 minutes; bake 2-inch for about 7 minutes. In either case, bake until the bottoms are lightly browned. Transfer to a wire rack and cool completely. Prepare Quick Cookie Icing (below). Spread icing on top of each cookie; sprinkle with crushed candy before the icing sets.

QUICK COOKIE ICING

INGREDIENTS

1	cup powdered sugar
1 to 2	tablespoons water

DIRECTIONS

In a 1-quart bowl, stir the sugar with enough water to reach a smooth, desired consistency.

STAMPED SHORTBREAD

Use silicone cookie stamps to impress buttery balls of dough with seasonal motifs.

This dough is wonderful and fun to work with, and the festive cookies are lusciously delicious.

- Makes about 2 dozen -

INGREDIENTS

2.4-inch silicone cookie stamps

Extra granulated sugar to coat balls of dough (about 3 tablespoons)

2 cups all-purpose flour

¼ cup cornstarch

1 cup (2 sticks) unsalted butter, softened

½ cup granulated sugar

DIRECTIONS

Preheat the oven to 350 degrees F.

Into a medium bowl, sift the flour with the cornstarch; whisk briefly. Set aside.

In a large bowl and with a mixer on medium speed, cream the butter until smooth, about 30 seconds. Gradually add ½ cup sugar and then beat until light and fluffy, 3 to 4 minutes. Reduce speed to low. Add the flour-cornstarch mixture in 4 or 5 parts, beating just until each addition is incorporated.

Put the extra granulated sugar into a small bowl. Use 1½ tablespoons of dough per cookie and shape into balls. Roll the balls in extra sugar to coat allover, and place about 2 inches apart on ungreased baking sheets. Firmly press each dough ball with a cookie stamp.

Bake for 10 to 15 minutes or until the bottoms are lightly browned. Transfer the cookies to a wire rack when they're firm enough to move. Cool completely.

YEAR-ROUND FAVORITES

What's your favorite cookie? Below, chocolate are listed first, followed by peanut, oatmeal, pecan and butter cookies. Among these types, you will find several tasty varieties—plus Snickerdoodles.

CHOCOLATE-CHUNK COCOA COOKIES

Use dark chocolate chunks or semisweet-chocolate chips in this double-chocolate recipe. Either way the cookies have outstanding flavor, and anyone who loves chocolate will love, love, love this cookie.

- Makes about 45 cookies -

INGREDIENTS

	Parchment paper
	Extra granulated sugar to flatten cookies (about 2 tablespoons)
1¾	cups all-purpose flour
⅓	cup natural (non-alkalized) unsweetened cocoa powder
½	teaspoon baking soda
¼	teaspoon salt
12	tablespoons (1½ sticks) unsalted butter, softened
1	cup firmly packed dark-brown sugar
½	cup granulated sugar
1	large egg
1½	teaspoons pure vanilla extract
1	cup dark chocolate chunks

DIRECTIONS

Preheat the oven to 350 degrees F.

Line baking sheets with parchment paper. Set aside.

Into a medium bowl, sift together the first 4 dry ingredients (flour through salt); whisk briefly. Set aside.

In a large bowl and with a mixer on medium speed, cream the butter for 30 seconds. Gradually add both sugars and then beat until well blended, 2 to 3 minutes. Beat in the egg and extract. Use a wooden spoon to stir in the flour mixture in 4 parts. Stir in the chocolate chunks.

Put the extra granulated sugar into a small bowl. Use 1 level tablespoon of dough per cookie and shape into balls. Place on the prepared baking sheets, spacing about 2 inches apart. Slightly flatten with the greased bottom of a drinking glass dipped into the extra granulated sugar.

Bake for 10 to 12 minutes or just until the edges of the cookies are firm and the centers are still soft. (Do not overbake.) Let cookies cool on the baking sheet until firm enough to move, about 2 minutes. Transfer to a wire rack and cool completely.

CHOCOLATE-COVERED RAISIN COOKIES

Dark chocolate, milk chocolate or even yogurt covered raisins work well here—whatever you like.

- Makes about 4 dozen -

INGREDIENTS

2	cups all-purpose flour
2	teaspoons ground cinnamon
1	teaspoon baking soda
1	teaspoon salt
1	cup (2 sticks) unsalted butter, softened
1	cup firmly packed light-brown sugar
½	cup granulated sugar
1	large egg
1	teaspoon pure vanilla extract
1½	cups chocolate-covered raisins

DIRECTIONS

Preheat the oven to 375 degrees F.

Into a medium bowl, sift together the first 4 dry ingredients (flour through salt); whisk briefly. Set aside.

In a large bowl and with a mixer on medium speed, cream the butter until smooth, about 30 seconds. Gradually add both sugars and then beat until light and fluffy, 4 to 5 minutes. Beat in the egg and extract. Use a wooden spoon to gradually stir in the flour mixture. Stir in the raisins.

Drop rounded tablespoons of dough onto ungreased baking sheets, spacing about 2 inches apart.

Bake for 10 to 12 minutes or until just golden brown. Cool cookies on the baking sheet until firm enough to move, about 2 minutes. Transfer to a wire rack and cool completely.

Note: Shiny-metal baking sheets are highly recommended.

CHOCOLATE MINT COOKIES

Actually, the special ingredient in this recipe—besides mint chocolate chips—is cream cheese. The cookie dough produces a very tender and mouthwatering foundation for the mint chips. Use cream de menthe baking chips to make the cookies even more special.

- Makes about 6 dozen -

INGREDIENTS

1	cup butter-flavored shortening, at room temperature
1	package (8 ounces) cream cheese, at room temperature
¾	cup granulated sugar
½	cup firmly packed light-brown sugar
1	teaspoon pure vanilla extract
2	cups all-purpose flour
1¾	cups mint chocolate chips

DIRECTIONS

Preheat the oven to 350 degrees F.

In a large bowl, combine the first 5 ingredients (shortening through extract). Beat with a mixer on medium speed until well combined and fluffy, about 2 minutes, scraping down the bowl with a rubber spatula as needed. Reduce speed to low. Gradually add the flour, mixing in each addition just until incorporated. Fold in chocolate chips with a rubber spatula.

Drop dough by level tablespoons onto ungreased baking sheets, spacing about 2 inches apart.

Bake for 8 to 10 minutes or until lightly browned. Transfer cookies to a wire rack when they are firm enough to move. Cool completely.

CHOCOLATE CHIP ORANGE DROPS

This is a soft and tender cookie with a wonderful, chocolaty-orange flavor.

- Makes about 3 dozen –

INGREDIENTS

	Extra butter to grease the baking sheets
½	cup (1 stick) unsalted butter, softened
3	ounces cream cheese, at room temperature
½	cup powdered sugar
1	large egg
1	teaspoon pure vanilla extract
¼	teaspoon salt
	Zest from 1 large navel orange*
1	cup all-purpose flour
1	cup semisweet chocolate chips

DIRECTIONS

Preheat the oven to 350 degrees F.

Lightly grease baking sheets. Set aside.

In a large bowl and with a mixer on medium speed, cream the butter with the cream cheese until smoothly blended. Gradually add the powdered sugar and then beat until light and fluffy, about 3 minutes. Beat in the egg, extract, salt, and zest. Reduce speed to low. Add the flour in 3 or 4 parts, mixing only until each addition is incorporated. Use a wooden spoon to stir in the chocolate chips.

Drop level tablespoons of dough onto the prepared baking sheets, spacing about 2 inches apart.

Bake for 10 to 12 minutes or until lightly browned on the bottoms and around the edges. Transfer cookies to a wire rack when firm enough to move, 2 to 3 minutes. Cool completely.

*See **Orange & Lemon Zest** (page XIII).

AMARETTO CHOCOLATE CHIP COOKIES

*The flavors of coconut, chocolate and almond combine to produce a cookie that tastes a lot like my favorite candy bar, ALMOND JOY. If you would like to use amaretto liqueur in another recipe, see **Almond-Chocolate Chip Cookies with Amaretto Frosting** (page 180).*

- Makes about 6 dozen -

INGREDIENTS

2½	cups all-purpose flour
1	teaspoon baking powder
1	teaspoon baking soda
½	teaspoon salt
1	cup (2 sticks) unsalted butter, softened
1	cup firmly packed light-brown sugar
½	cup granulated sugar
2	large eggs
1	tablespoon amaretto liqueur
2	teaspoons pure almond extract
2	cups semisweet chocolate chips
1	cup sweetened flaked coconut
1	cup sliced almonds

DIRECTIONS

Preheat the oven to 375 degrees F.

Into a medium bowl, sift together the first 4 dry ingredients (flour through salt); whisk briefly. Set aside.

In a large bowl and with a mixer on medium speed, cream the butter until smooth, about 30 seconds. Gradually add both sugars; beat until light and fluffy, 4 to 5 minutes. Beat in the eggs one at a time; beat in the liqueur and extract. Reduce speed to low. Add the flour mixture in 4 parts; beat until each addition is just incorporated. Use a wooden spoon to stir in the chocolate chips, coconut, and nuts.

Drop rounded tablespoons of dough onto ungreased baking sheets, spacing about 2 inches apart.

Bake for 9 to 10 minutes or until golden around the edges. Allow cookies to cool on the sheet for 2 to 3 minutes and then transfer to a wire rack. Cool completely.

> **Note:** Use shiny-metal baking sheets; these cookies brown too quickly on dark, non-stick sheets.

CHOCOLATE CHIP BUNDLES

I love this recipe for its elegant simplicity. Beloved component flavors of buttery sweetness, vanilla, chocolate and walnuts are easily discernible and evenly balanced in every bite of this lovely cookie.

- Makes about 2 dozen –

INGREDIENTS

½	cup (1 stick) unsalted butter, softened
3	tablespoons firmly packed light-brown sugar
1	teaspoon pure vanilla extract
1	cup all-purpose flour
⅔	cup semisweet chocolate chips
½	cup coarsely chopped walnuts

DIRECTIONS

Preheat the oven to 350 degrees F.

In a large bowl and with a mixer on medium speed, cream the butter until smooth. Add the brown sugar and beat until very well blended. Beat in the extract. Use a wooden spoon to gradually stir in the flour. Stir in the chocolate chips and nuts.

Drop dough by rounded tablespoons onto ungreased baking sheets, spacing about 2 inches apart.

Bake for 15 minutes or until lightly browned. Cool the cookies on the baking sheet until firm enough to move. Transfer to a wire rack and cool completely.

Note: If desired, roll the thoroughly cooled cookies in powdered sugar to coat allover.

CHOCOLATE CHIP-MACADAMIA NUT COOKIES

Once you taste this cookie, ordinary chocolate chip cookies will rarely satisfy.

- Makes about 7 dozen -

INGREDIENTS

2¼	cups all-purpose flour
1	teaspoon baking soda
¾	teaspoon salt
1	cup (2 sticks) unsalted butter, softened
¾	cup firmly packed light-brown sugar
¾	cup granulated sugar
2	large eggs
1	teaspoon pure vanilla extract
2	cups semisweet chocolate chips
1	cup vanilla baking chips (see Note page 75)
2	cups coarsely chopped macadamia nuts

DIRECTIONS

Into a medium bowl, sift together the flour, baking soda, and salt; whisk briefly. Set aside.

In a large bowl and with a mixer on medium speed, cream the butter until smooth, about 30 seconds. Gradually add both sugars and then beat until light and fluffy, about 4 minutes. Beat in the eggs one at a time; beat in the extract. Reduce speed to low. Beat in the flour mixture in 4 parts, just until each addition is incorporated. Use a wooden spoon to stir in the chocolate and vanilla chips. Stir in the nuts. Cover and refrigerate for at least 4 hours or overnight.

Preheat the oven to 375 degrees F.

The dough will be quite stiff. If desired, let it stand at room temperature for 30+ minutes for easier handling. Drop rounded tablespoons of dough onto ungreased baking sheets, spacing about 2 inches apart.

Bake for 10 to 12 minutes or just until lightly browned. (Do not overbake.) Transfer the cookies to a wire rack when they are firm enough to move. Cool completely.

> **Note:** Use shiny-metal baking sheets to produce light-golden-brown cookies without a hint of burnt flavor.

PEANUT BUTTER-CHOCOLATE CHIP COOKIES

There's crisp rice cereal and oatmeal in this recipe. The cereals add an interesting texture, and the cookies are soft in the center and firm-crisp around the edges. Double ingredients to make a big batch.

- Makes about 3 dozen –

INGREDIENTS

¾	cup all-purpose flour
¼	teaspoon baking powder
¼	teaspoon baking soda
½	teaspoon salt
4	tablespoons (½ stick) unsalted butter, softened
¼	cup peanut butter (creamy or crunchy)
½	cup granulated sugar
¼	cup firmly packed light-brown sugar
½	tablespoon light corn syrup
1	large egg
1	teaspoon pure vanilla extract
½	cup dry rolled oats (quick cooking or old fashioned, not instant)
½	cup crisp rice cereal
1	cup semisweet chocolate chips

DIRECTIONS

Preheat the oven to 350 degrees F.

Into a medium bowl, sift together the first 4 dry ingredients (flour through salt); whisk briefly. Set aside.

In a large bowl and with a mixer on medium speed, cream the butter with the peanut butter until smoothly blended. Gradually add both sugars and then beat until very well combined. Beat in the corn syrup, egg, and extract. Reduce speed to low. Add the flour mixture in 3 parts, beating just until each addition is incorporated. Use a wooden spoon to stir in the cereals and chocolate chips.

Drop dough by level tablespoons onto ungreased baking sheets, spacing about 2 inches apart.

Bake for about 10 minutes or until light golden brown. Cool on the baking sheet until firm enough to move, about 2 minutes. Transfer cookies to a wire rack and cool completely.

> **Note:** Shiny-metal baking sheets work best here.

63

SALTED PEANUT-CHOCOLATE CHIP COOKIES

A delightful variation on a basic chocolate-chip-cookie recipe—it includes more nuts and less chocolate. The recipe easily doubles to make about 6 dozen delicious nutty cookies.

- Makes about 3 dozen -

INGREDIENTS

	Granulated sugar to flatten cookies (about 2 tablespoons)
1½	cups all-purpose flour
¼	teaspoon baking soda
4	tablespoons (½ stick) unsalted butter, softened
4	tablespoons shortening, at room temperature
¾	cup firmly packed light-brown sugar
1	large egg
1	teaspoon pure vanilla extract
1	cup peanuts with sea salt
½	cup semisweet chocolate chips

DIRECTIONS

Preheat the oven to 375 degrees F.

Into a medium bowl, sift the flour with the baking soda; whisk briefly. Set aside.

In a large bowl and with a mixer on medium speed, beat the butter with the shortening until smoothly blended. Gradually add the brown sugar and then beat until very well combined. Beat in the egg and extract. Reduce speed to low. Gradually beat in as much flour as you can with the mixer; stir in remaining flour with a wooden spoon. Stir in the nuts and chocolate chips.

Put the granulated sugar into a small bowl. Use 1 level tablespoon of dough per cookie and shape into balls. Space about 2 inches apart on ungreased baking sheets. Slightly flatten with the greased bottom of a drinking glass dipped into the granulated sugar.

Bake for 8 to 10 minutes or until barely brown. Let the cookies cool on the baking sheet until firm enough to move, about 2 minutes. Transfer to a wire rack and cool completely.

PEANUT DELIGHTS

This recipe offers an interesting departure from ordinary peanut butter cookies. However, if you really want a traditional cookie, consider non-traditional **Flourless Peanut Butter Cookies** *(page 190).*

- Makes about 3 dozen –

INGREDIENTS

	About 2 ounces bittersweet chocolate, melted for drizzle
1	very full cup of unsalted dry-roasted peanuts (5 ounces)
¾	cup all-purpose flour
1	teaspoon baking powder
½	cup (1 stick) unsalted butter, softened
¾	cup granulated sugar
1	large egg

DIRECTIONS

Preheat the oven to 375 degrees F.

In a food processor (or see Note below), pulse the nuts until finely ground. Set aside.

Into a medium bowl, sift the flour with the baking powder; whisk briefly. Set aside.

In a large bowl and with a mixer on medium speed, cream the butter. Gradually beat in the sugar and then beat until very well blended. Beat in the egg. Use a wooden spoon to stir in the ground peanuts. Stir in the flour mixture in 3 or 4 parts just until each addition is incorporated.

Drop level tablespoons of dough onto ungreased baking sheets, spacing about 2 inches apart.

Bake for about 8 minutes or until golden brown. Cool cookies on the baking sheet for 2 minutes. Transfer to a wire rack and cool completely. Drizzle lightly with melted chocolate.

Note: TO FINELY GRIND NUTS such as peanuts, almonds, pecans, or hazelnuts (filberts), a coffee grinder works great. In my kitchen, I keep an electric grinder that's dedicated to baking projects. It's so easy. Simply grind nuts in small batches. To clean the appliance, pulse pieces of stale bread. The bread picks up leftover grinds and absorbs oil and dust. Then dump out the bread and thoroughly wipe the interior with a damp paper towel.

CLASSIC CHEWY OATMEAL COOKIES

Enjoy the sweet brown-sugar, vanilla-cinnamon flavor of this cookie—it's perfection. Use only pure vanilla extract, here and always. Avoid imitation vanilla at all costs; it has a contrived, harsh-chemical flavor that barely resembles the pure extract. Classic oatmeal cookies deserve the best.

- Makes about 4 dozen -

INGREDIENTS

	Extra shortening to grease the baking sheets
1	cup all-purpose flour
½	teaspoon baking soda
½	teaspoon salt
½	teaspoon ground cinnamon
3	cups dry quick-cooking rolled oats (not instant or old fashioned)
¾	cup butter-flavored shortening, at room temperature
1¼	cups firmly packed light-brown sugar
1	large egg
⅓	cup milk (whole tastes best)
1½	teaspoons pure vanilla extract
1	cup raisins
1	cup coarsely chopped walnuts

DIRECTIONS

Preheat the oven to 375 degrees F.

Lightly grease baking sheets. Set aside.

Into a large bowl, sift together the flour, baking soda, salt, and cinnamon. Whisk in the oats. Set aside.

In another large bowl, combine the shortening, brown sugar, egg, milk, and extract. Beat with a mixer on medium speed until well blended. Reduce speed to low. Add the dry ingredients in 4 parts, mixing just until each addition is incorporated. Use a wooden spoon to stir in the raisins and nuts.

Drop dough by rounded tablespoons onto the prepared baking sheets, spacing about 2 inches apart.

Bake for 10 to 12 minutes or until just lightly browned. Cool on the baking sheets until firm enough to move, about 2 minutes. Transfer cookies to a wire rack and cool completely.

69

WHOLE-WHEAT OATMEAL COOKIES

An optional cinnamon-sugar topping enlivens the flavor of this cookie. The recipe includes no eggs, but it uses buttermilk. If you have none on hand, make your own buttermilk substitution (see Note below).

- Makes about 5½ dozen –

INGREDIENTS

1¾   cups whole-wheat flour

1   teaspoon baking soda

½   teaspoon salt

1   cup shortening, at room temperature

2   cups firmly packed brown sugar, light or dark (I prefer dark or a combo of both)

½   cup buttermilk

1   teaspoon pure vanilla extract

4   cups dry quick-cooking rolled oats (not instant or old-fashioned)

     CINNAMON SUGAR (optional—see page 93)

DIRECTIONS

Preheat the oven to 375 degrees F.

Into a medium bowl, sift together the whole-wheat flour, baking soda, and salt; whisk briefly. Set aside.

In a large bowl, combine the shortening, brown sugar, buttermilk, and vanilla. Beat with a mixer on medium speed until well blended. Reduce speed to low. Gradually add the flour mixture. Stir in the oats with a wooden spoon.

If using, prepare Cinnamon Sugar in a shallow bowl.

Use 1 level tablespoon of dough per cookie and shape into balls. If desired, roll balls in cinnamon sugar to coat the top and sides—leave the bottoms naked. Space balls about 2 inches apart on ungreased baking sheets. Slightly flatten with a fork.

Bake for 8 to 10 minutes or until just golden brown. Transfer cookies to a wire rack; cool completely.

> **Note:** TO MAKE A BUTTERMILK SUBSTITUTION, put 1½ teaspoons lemon juice or white vinegar into a glass measuring cup. Add enough milk to equal ½ cup. Stir, and then let the mixture stand a few minutes to thicken.

OATMEAL-APPLESAUCE COOKIES

Here's a soft oatmeal cookie that's fruity, satisfying and delicious. Instead of chopping walnuts, break up walnut halves with your fingertips. This produces larger pieces of nuts that are extra satiating.

If desired, add extra nuts.

- Makes about 5 dozen -

INGREDIENTS

2	cups all-purpose flour
1	teaspoon ground cinnamon
½	teaspoon baking soda
½	teaspoon salt
¾	cup shortening, at room temperature
1	cup firmly packed light-brown sugar
1	large egg
1	teaspoon pure vanilla extract
1	cup unsweetened applesauce
1½	cups dry quick-cooking rolled oats (not instant or old-fashioned)
½	cup raisins
½	cup chopped walnuts

DIRECTIONS

Preheat the oven to 375 degrees F.

Into a medium bowl, sift together the first 4 dry ingredients (flour through salt); whisk briefly. Set aside.

In a large bowl, combine the shortening, brown sugar, egg, extract, and applesauce. Beat with a mixer on medium speed until very well combined. Reduce speed to low. Add the flour mixture in 3 or 4 parts. Use a wooden spoon to stir in the oats. Stir in the raisins and nuts.

Drop the dough by rounded tablespoons onto ungreased baking sheets, spacing about 2 inches apart.

Bake for 12 to 15 minutes or until lightly browned. Let the cookies cool on the baking sheet for 2 to 3 minutes and then transfer to a wire rack. Cool completely.

OATMEAL COOKIES WITH APRICOT & VANILLA CHIPS

Nearly thirty years ago, I clipped this recipe out of a magazine and made it for our neighborhood block party. I piled the cookies into a large plastic bowl. In the evening, we sat in a circle and talked as we passed the bowl from person to person—a very nice memory and a great cookie.

- Makes about 6½ dozen –

INGREDIENTS

Extra granulated sugar to flatten cookies (about 2 tablespoons)

1½ cups all-purpose flour—plus 1 tablespoon, divided use

1 teaspoon baking soda

¾ teaspoon salt

1 cup butter-flavored shortening, at room temperature

1 cup firmly packed light-brown sugar

1 cup granulated sugar

2 large eggs

1 teaspoon pure vanilla extract

2½ cups dry rolled oats (quick-cooking or old-fashioned, not instant)

1 cup chopped hazelnuts or walnuts

1 cup chopped dried apricots

1 cup vanilla baking chips

DIRECTIONS

Preheat the oven to 350 degrees F.

Into a medium bowl, sift 1½ cups flour with the baking soda and salt; whisk briefly. Set aside.

In a large bowl, combine the shortening, both sugars, eggs, and extract. Beat with a mixer on medium speed until blended, about 3 minutes. Use a wooden spoon to stir in the flour mixture in 3 parts. Stir in the oats and nuts. Put the apricots into a 1-quart bowl; add the remaining 1 tablespoon flour and toss to evenly coat. Stir the fruit into the dough; stir in the vanilla chips.

Put the extra granulated sugar into a small bowl. Use 1 rounded tablespoon of dough per cookie and shape into balls. Space about 2 inches apart on ungreased baking sheets. Slightly flatten with the greased bottom of a drinking glass dipped into the extra sugar.

Bake for 11 to 13 minutes or until just beginning to brown around the edges and the center is still a bit moist. Immediately, transfer cookies to a wire rack and cool completely.

> **Note:** USE GHIRARDELLI CLASSIC WHITE BAKING CHIPS; they are made with real vanilla extract and have very good overall aroma and flavor.

MOM'S RANGER COOKIES

These cookies often go by the name of California Rangers, and in the recipe Mom clipped from the newspaper—decades ago—it included cornflakes. Mom replaced the flakes with crisp rice cereal, doubled the vanilla and used dates instead of raisins. The recipe makes a large batch, but you can easily reduce it by half, if so inclined.

- Makes about 7 dozen -

INGREDIENTS

	Extra shortening to grease the baking sheets	2	large eggs
2	cups all-purpose flour	2	teaspoons pure vanilla extract
1	teaspoon baking soda	2	cups dry rolled oats (quick-cooking or old-fashioned, not instant)
½	teaspoon baking powder		
½	teaspoon salt		
1	cup butter-flavored shortening, at room temperature	2	cups crisp rice cereal
		1	cup sweetened flaked coconut
1	cup firmly packed light-brown sugar	1	cup chopped dates
		1	cup chopped walnuts
1	cup granulated sugar		

DIRECTIONS

Preheat the oven to 375 degrees F.

Lightly grease baking sheets. Set aside.

Into a medium bowl, sift the first 4 dry ingredients (flour through salt); whisk briefly. Set aside.

In a large bowl and with a mixer on medium speed, thoroughly cream the shortening with both sugars. Beat in the eggs one at a time; beat in the extract. Reduce speed to low. Beat in the flour mixture in 3 or 4 parts. Use a wooden spoon to stir in the oats, rice cereal, coconut, dates, and nuts.

Drop dough by rounded tablespoons onto the prepared baking sheets, spacing about 2 inches apart.

Bake for 10 to 12 minutes or until lightly browned. Transfer cookies to a wire rack; cool completely.

MULTIGRAIN COOKIES

Here's a versatile recipe, and a cookie I keep stashed in the freezer for myself. Sometimes I skip the butter and use eight tablespoons of shortening. Other times, instead of almond butter and almonds, I use peanut butter and peanuts. If you like, substitute raisins for dates or use no fruit.

- Makes about 3½ dozen –

INGREDIENTS

1	cup whole-wheat flour
½	teaspoon baking powder
½	teaspoon baking soda
6	tablespoons oat bran
2	tablespoons wheat germ
¼	cup dry quick-cooking rolled oats (not instant or old-fashioned)
4	tablespoons (½ stick) unsalted butter, softened
4	tablespoons shortening, at room temperature
½	cup almond butter
1	cup firmly packed light-brown sugar
1	large egg
1	teaspoon pure vanilla extract
½	cup sliced or slivered almonds (a combo of sliced and slivered boosts texture)
½	cup chopped dates

DIRECTIONS

Preheat the oven to 375 degrees F.

Into a medium bowl, sift together the whole-wheat flour, baking powder, and baking soda. Whisk in the oat bran, wheat germ, and oats. Set aside.

In a large bowl and with a mixer on medium speed, cream together the butter, shortening, and almond butter until smoothly blended. Gradually add the brown sugar; beat until well combined. Beat in the egg and extract. Use a wooden spoon to stir in the dry ingredients in 4 parts. Stir in the nuts and dates.

Use 1 level tablespoon of dough per cookie and squeeze into balls. (The dough tends to be crumbly but will hold together as it bakes.) Space balls about 2 inches apart on ungreased baking sheets.

Bake for 9 to 10 minutes or just until the cookies are set and begin to brown. Cool on the baking sheet until firm enough to move, 2 to 3 minutes. Transfer to a wire rack and cool completely.

TOASTED PECAN CRISPS

This is a brown-sugar butter cookie made extra rich by the addition of pecans—toasted. Use either dark or light-brown sugar. Dark-brown sugar contains more molasses and contributes more robust flavor. If desired, double the ingredients for a larger yield.

- Makes about 3 dozen -

INGREDIENTS

	Granulate sugar to flatten cookies (about 2 tablespoons)
½	cup chopped pecans
1½	cups all-purpose flour
¼	teaspoon baking soda
½	cup (1 stick) unsalted butter, softened
1¼	cups firmly packed brown sugar (light or dark, your choice)
1	large egg
½	teaspoon pure vanilla extract

DIRECTIONS

Toast the nuts (see Note page 17). Set aside and cool to room temperature.

Preheat the oven to 375 degrees F.

Into a 1-quart bowl, sift the flour with the baking soda; whisk briefly. Set aside.

In a large bowl and with a mixer on medium speed, cream the butter. Gradually add the brown sugar and then beat until well blended. Beat in the egg and extract. Use a wooden spoon to stir in the flour mixture in 4 parts. Stir in the toasted nuts.

Put the granulated sugar into a small bowl. Use 1 level tablespoon of dough per cookie and shape into balls. Space about 2 inches apart on ungreased baking sheets. Flatten to about a ⅛-inch thickness with the greased bottom of a drinking glass dipped into the granulated sugar.

Bake for 8 to 10 minutes or until the edges are light golden brown. Cool on the baking sheet for 1 to 2 minutes. Transfer cookies to a wire rack and cool completely.

ESPRESSO-PECAN COOKIES

Prepare yourself for the delicious flavor of strong coffee, thanks to the use of instant espresso powder. If you would like to use espresso powder in other recipes see the following: **Rum-Espresso Cookies** *(page 40),* **Mocha-Pecan Cookies** *(page 86),* **Mocha-Almond Bars** *(page 144), and* **Oatmeal Cookies with Espresso Frosting** *(page 178).*

- Makes about 34 cookies –

INGREDIENTS

2	cups all-purpose flour
2	teaspoons instant espresso powder
¼	teaspoon salt
1	cup (2 sticks) unsalted butter, softened
½	cup granulated sugar
	About 1 cup chopped pecans

DIRECTIONS

Preheat the oven to 300 degrees F.

Into a medium bowl, sift together the flour, espresso powder, and salt; whisk briefly. Set aside.

In a large bowl and with a mixer on medium speed, cream the butter until smooth, about 30 seconds. Gradually add the sugar and then beat until light and fluffy, 3 to 4 minutes. Reduce speed to low.

Slowly add the flour mixture, beating in as much as you can with the mixer. Stir in remaining flour with a wooden spoon.

Put nuts into a shallow bowl. Use 1 level tablespoon of dough per cookie and shape into balls. Roll each ball in nuts to coat allover. Space about 2 inches apart on ungreased baking sheets.

Bake for about 20 minutes or until the edges are lightly browned. Transfer cookies to a wire rack and cool completely.

PECAN PUFFS

The recipe below may seems simple, but it truly produces an outstanding result.

Thanks to cake flour, the cookies have an extra-tender texture.

- Makes about 2 dozen -

INGREDIENTS

	Powdered sugar for dusting (about 1 tablespoon)
½	cup (1 stick) unsalted butter, softened
2	tablespoons granulated sugar
1	teaspoon pure vanilla extract
1	cup cake flour
1	cup chopped pecans

DIRECTIONS

Preheat the oven to 300 degrees F.

In a large bowl and with a mixer on medium speed, cream the butter. Add the granulated sugar and beat until very well blended. Beat in the extract. With a rubber spatula or wooden spoon, stir in the cake flour in 4 parts; stir just until each addition is incorporated. Stir in the nuts.

Use 1 level tablespoon of dough per cookie and shape into balls. Space about 2 inches apart on ungreased baking sheets.

Bake for 30 minutes or until the bottoms are golden brown. Transfer cookies to a wire rack and cool. Dust with powdered sugar dredged through a fine-mesh sieve.

Note: Use dark, non-stick baking sheets for golden brown bottoms in about 30 minutes of baking time. If using shiny-metal sheets, the cookies will have to bake a few additional minutes.

MOCHA-PECAN COOKIES

Espresso powder and cocoa combine to produce the flavor of mocha. The recipe includes a powdered sugar dusting of the finished cookies, however the flavor is quite delicious without any added sweetness. Try it both ways and see what you think.

- Makes about 45 cookies –

INGREDIENTS

	Powdered sugar for dusting (about 1 tablespoon)
1¾	cups all-purpose flour
¼	cup natural (non-alkalized) unsweetened cocoa powder
2	teaspoons instant espresso powder
½	teaspoon salt
1	cup (2 sticks) unsalted butter, softened
½	cup granulated sugar
2	teaspoons pure vanilla extract
2	cups finely chopped pecans

DIRECTIONS

Preheat the oven to 325 degrees F.

Into a medium bowl, sift together the first 4 dry ingredients (flour through salt); whisk briefly. Set aside.

In a large bowl and with a mixer on medium speed, cream the butter until smooth, about 30 seconds. Gradually add the granulated sugar; beat until light and fluffy, 3 to 4 minutes. Beat in the extract.

Reduce speed to low. Gradually add the flour mixture, beating in as much as you can with the mixer. Stir in remaining flour with a wooden spoon. Stir in the nuts.

Use 1 level tablespoon of dough per cookie and shape into balls. Space about 2 inches apart on ungreased baking sheets.

Bake for 15 minutes. Cool cookies on the baking sheet until firm enough to move, about 4 minutes. Transfer to a wire rack and cool completely. If desired, dust with a bit of powdered sugar dredged through a fine-mesh sieve.

COCONUT BUTTER COOKIES

This is a very buttery-thin cookie. The coconut flavor is subtle and intermittent. I make these cookies both big and small. When larger, the cookies are soft in the center and crisp along the edges; smaller cookies are crisp throughout. I include both when making a batch. This adds variety to my eating pleasure, and people can choose the size and texture they like best.

- Makes about 6 dozen small or 3 dozen large cookies -

INGREDIENTS

	Extra granulated sugar to flatten cookies (about 2 tablespoons)
1½	cups all-purpose flour
½	teaspoon baking soda
¼	teaspoon salt
1	cup (2 sticks) unsalted butter, softened
1	cup granulated sugar
½	teaspoon pure vanilla extract
½	cup sweetened flaked coconut

DIRECTIONS

Preheat the oven to 350 degrees F.

Into a 1-quart bowl, sift together the flour, baking soda, and salt; whisk briefly. Set aside.

In a large bowl and with a mixer on medium speed, cream the butter until smooth, about 30 seconds. Gradually add 1 cup sugar; beat until light and fluffy, 4 to 5 minutes. Beat in the extract. Use a wooden spoon to stir in the dry ingredients in 4 parts, stirring only until each addition is incorporated. Stir in the coconut.

Use either a 1-tablespoon measure for large cookies or a ½-tablespoon measure for small cookies. (If making both sizes at once, use separate sheets and bake separately.) Heap dough into the measuring spoon with a butter knife and level off at the rim. Scoop the dough out and drop onto ungreased baking sheets, spacing about 2 inches apart. Shape each mound of dough into a ball; place back on the sheet.

Put the extra granulated sugar into a small bowl. Slightly flatten balls with the greased bottom of a drinking glass dipped into the extra sugar.

Bake small cookies for about 8 minutes; large cookies for about 10. In either case, bake until the edges are just golden brown. Transfer cookies to a wire rack when firm enough to move. Cool completely.

SUNNY CITRUS COOKIES

Make either orange or lemon cookies by switching the extracts and citrus zest—or combine both flavors.

- Makes about 3½ dozen -

INGREDIENTS

Parchment paper

Extra granulated sugar to flatten cookies (about 2 tablespoons)

2 cups all-purpose flour, plus 2 tablespoons

½ teaspoon cream of tartar

½ teaspoon baking soda

½ teaspoon salt

½ cup (1 stick) unsalted butter, softened

½ cup powdered sugar

½ cup granulated sugar

1 large egg

½ cup canola or corn oil

½ teaspoon pure lemon or orange extract

Shaved zest of one large lemon or navel orange*

DIRECTIONS

Into a medium bowl, sift the first 4 dry ingredients (flour through salt); whisk briefly. Set aside.

In a large bowl and with a mixer on medium speed, cream the butter. Gradually add both sugars; beat until fluffy. Beat in the egg. Add the oil in 4 parts. Beat in the extract and zest. Reduce speed to low. Gradually add the flour mixture. (The dough will be very soft.) Cover the bowl; refrigerate overnight.

Next day, preheat the oven to 325 degrees F.

Line baking sheets with parchment paper.

Put the extra sugar into a small bowl. Use 1 level tablespoon of dough per cookie and shape into balls. (Keep the dough cold; work with small portions.) Place balls 2½ inches apart on the prepared sheets. Flatten into 2-inch circles with the greased bottom of a drinking glass dipped into the extra sugar.

Bake for 8 to 10 minutes or just until slightly golden around the edges. Let the cookies cool on the baking sheet for 2 to 3 minutes. Transfer to a wire rack and cool completely.

*See **Orange & Lemon Zest** (page XIII).

SNICKERDOODLES

A New England classic, balls of cookie dough are rolled in a sugary-cinnamon mixture and then baked. The name is thought to have originated from a German word meaning "crinkly noodles."

- Makes about 5 dozen -

INGREDIENTS

2¾	cups all-purpose flour
2	teaspoons cream of tartar
1	teaspoon baking soda
¼	teaspoon salt
½	cup (1 stick) unsalted butter, softened
½	cup (8 tablespoons) shortening, at room temperature
1½	cups granulated sugar
2	large eggs

DIRECTIONS

Preheat the oven to 400 degrees F.

Into a medium bowl, sift the first 4 dry ingredients (flour through salt); whisk briefly. Set aside.

In a large bowl and with a mixer on medium speed, cream together the butter and shortening until smoothly blended. Gradually add 1½ cups sugar and then beat until light and fluffy, about 4 minutes. Beat in the eggs one at a time. Reduce speed to low. Gradually add the flour mixture, beating just until each addition is incorporated.

Prepare Cinnamon Sugar (below).

Use 1 level tablespoon of dough per cookie and shape into balls. Roll the balls in the cinnamon-sugar mixture to coat allover. Space about 2 inches apart on ungreased baking sheets.

Bake for 8 to 10 minutes or until set. Transfer cookies to a wire rack and cool completely.

CINNAMON SUGAR

INGREDIENTS

| ¼ | cup granulated sugar |
| 4 | teaspoons ground cinnamon |

DIRECTIONS

Simply combine the sugar and cinnamon in a shallow bowl.

WEDDING CAKE COOKIES

Variations of the "wedding cake cookie" go by different names. All are special enough for any celebration just about anywhere. Actually, the cookie has several international versions. The basic ingredients include butter (no substitutions), powdered sugar, flour and nuts. Variant types come about with different proportions of the basic ingredients, the use of extracts, a bit of spice such as cinnamon or cardamom, the type of nut used and nut toasting, or even a pop of flavor from anise seed. All are extraordinarily delicious and merit space in any cookie collection.

Viennese Almond Crescents (page 8) actually fits this category, too.

MEXICAN WEDDING CAKE COOKIES

Known as Pastelitas de Boda—or little wedding cakes—these elegant pecan cookies are traditionally served in Mexico at weddings. Although, just about any occasion will seem extra special when these cookies are present.

- Makes about 3 dozen -

INGREDIENTS

	Extra powdered sugar to coat cookies (about ½ cup)
1	cup (2 sticks) unsalted butter, softened
½	cup powdered sugar
¼	teaspoon salt
1	teaspoon pure vanilla extract
2	cups all-purpose flour
1	cup finely chopped pecans

DIRECTIONS

Preheat the oven to 350 degrees F.

In a large bowl and with a mixer on medium speed, cream the butter until smooth, about 30 seconds. Gradually add ½ cup powdered sugar; add the salt and extract. Beat until very well blended and fluffy, 3 to 4 minutes. Reduce speed to low. Gradually add the flour, beating in as much as you can with the mixer. Stir in remaining flour with a wooden spoon. Stir in the nuts.

Use 1 level tablespoon of dough per cookie and shape into balls. Space about 2 inches apart on ungreased baking sheets.

Bake for 12 to 15 minutes or until the bottoms are golden brown. Transfer cookies to a wire rack when firm enough to move; cool completely. Meanwhile, put the extra powdered sugar into a shallow bowl.

Roll the cooled cookies in extra powdered sugar to coat allover.

SOUTHWEST ANISE COOKIES

Anise seeds, cinnamon and vanilla combine to produce an out-of-the-ordinary flavor.

If the anise seed is omitted, the cookies are still exceptionally delicious.

- Makes about 4 dozen –

INGREDIENTS

	Extra powdered sugar to flatten cookies and for dusting (about 2 tablespoons)
1¾	cups all-purpose flour
1	teaspoon anise seeds
½	teaspoon ground cinnamon
1¼	cups finely chopped walnuts
1	cup (2 sticks) unsalted butter, softened
1¼	cups powdered sugar
1	teaspoon pure vanilla extract

DIRECTIONS

Preheat the oven to 350 degrees F.

In a medium bowl, thoroughly whisk together the flour, anise seeds, and cinnamon. Whisk in the nuts. Set aside.

In a large bowl and with a mixer on medium speed, cream the butter until smooth, about 30 seconds. Gradually add 1¼ cups powdered sugar and then beat until very light and fluffy, about 4 minutes. Beat in the extract. Reduce speed to low. Add the flour mixture in 4 parts, beating in as much as you can with the mixer. Stir in any remaining flour with a wooden spoon.

Use 1 level tablespoon of dough per cookie and shape into balls. Space about 2 inches apart on ungreased baking sheets. Flatten the balls with fork tines dipped into the extra powdered sugar.

Bake for 12 to 15 minutes or until golden brown around the edges. As soon as the cookies are firm enough to move, transfer to a wire rack and cool completely. Lightly dust with extra sugar dredged through a fine-mesh sieve.

SWEDISH HEIRLOOM COOKIES

Originally, this recipe included a 5-ounce can of diced toasted almonds. That was decades ago and the ingredient isn't available today. So I use slivered almonds—toasted. You may dice the nuts if you like, but the cookie's texture is really more interesting when the slivered pieces are left whole.

- Makes about 40 cookies -

INGREDIENTS

	Extra powdered sugar to coat cookies, twice (about 1 cup)
1¼	cups (5 ounces) slivered almonds
1	cup (2 sticks) unsalted butter, softened
1	cup powdered sugar
½	teaspoon salt
1	tablespoon pure vanilla extract
2	cups all-purpose flour

DIRECTIONS

Toast the nuts (see Note page 17). Set aside and cool to room temperature.

Preheat the oven to 325 degrees F.

In a large bowl and with a mixer on medium speed, cream the butter until smooth, about 30 seconds. Gradually add 1 cup powdered sugar and beat until light and fluffy, 3 to 4 minutes. Beat in the salt and extract. Reduced speed to low. Gradually add the flour, beating in as much as you can with the mixer. Stir in remaining flour with a wooden spoon. Stir in the nuts.

Use 1 level tablespoon of dough per cookie and shape into balls. Space about 2 inches apart on ungreased baking sheets. Slightly flatten the balls, using the greased bottom of a drinking glass.

Bake for 15 to 18 minutes or until set and lightly browned on the bottoms. Meanwhile, put the extra powdered sugar into a shallow bowl.

As soon as the cookies are firm enough to move and still warm, roll in the extra sugar to cover allover. Place cookies on a wire rack and cool completely. Then double coat—roll again in powdered sugar to coat allover.

RUSSIAN TEA CAKES

Years ago during the holidays, a family friend brought me what looked like a plate piled with powdered sugar. Underneath were the most delicious buttery cookie-balls. The cookies had been double rolled in powdered sugar, once while still hot from the oven and again after cooling. Then the cookies were generously dredged with more powdered sugar—on the plate. Here's the recipe, enjoy.

- Makes about 3 dozen –

INGREDIENTS

Extra powdered sugar to coat cookies, twice—plus dust (about 1½ cups)

1	cup (2 sticks) unsalted butter, softened
½	cup powdered sugar
1	teaspoon pure vanilla extract
2	cups all-purpose flour
¾	cup finely chopped walnuts

DIRECTIONS

Preheat the oven to 400 degrees F.

In a large bowl and with a mixer on medium speed, cream the butter for 30 seconds. Gradually add ½ cup powdered sugar and then beat on high speed until very light and fluffy, 4 to 5 minutes. Beat in the extract. Reduce speed to low. Gradually add the flour, beating in as much as you can with the mixer. Stir in remaining flour with a wooden spoon just until incorporated. Stir in the nuts.

Use 1 level tablespoon of dough per cookie and shape into balls. Space about 2 inches apart on ungreased baking sheets.

Bake for about 10 minutes or until the cookies are lightly browned around the edges. Meanwhile, put the extra powdered sugar into a shallow bowl.

Immediately, roll hot cookies in the extra sugar to coat entirely and then place on a wire rack to cool completely. When thoroughly cool, roll in powdered sugar again.

To serve, arrange cookies on a plate (or in a shallow bowl) and dust liberally with more powdered sugar dredged through a fine-mesh sieve.

> **Note:** Watch the baking time carefully if using dark, non-stick sheets; the cookies brown faster on dark sheets. If using shiny-metal sheets, the baking time may have to increase 1 to 2 minutes to brown perfectly.

CHINESE NEW–YEAR NUT BALLS

Ground almonds play a big role in this recipe. Grind the nuts if you like, or substitute raw almond flour. To use the flour in other recipes, see **Almond Spritz** *(page 24),* **Almond Half-Moon Refrigerator Cookies** *(page 166),* **Gluten-Free Lemon-Almond Cookies** *(page 196),* **Gluten-Free Coconut Drops** *(page 198), and* **My Favorite Granola Bars** *(page 212). For more about almond flour, see page IX.*

- Makes about 1½ dozen -

INGREDIENTS

1   cup all-purpose flour
⅓   cup finely ground almonds* (or substitute ⅓ cup raw almond
            flour)
½   teaspoon ground cardamom
¼   teaspoon salt
½   cup (1 stick) unsalted butter, softened
½   cup powdered sugar
½   teaspoon pure almond extract

DIRECTIONS

Preheat the oven to 325 degrees F.

In a medium bowl, thoroughly whisk the all-purpose flour with the ground almonds (or almond flour), ½ teaspoon cardamom, and salt. Set aside.

In a large bowl and with a mixer on medium speed, cream the butter. Add ½ cup powdered sugar; beat until very well blended. Beat in the extract. Use a wooden spoon to gradually stir in the flour mixture.

Use 1 level tablespoon of dough per cookie and shape into balls or—if preferred—logs, bending midway to form a crescent shape. Space about 1½ inches apart on ungreased baking sheets.

Bake for 18 to 20 minutes or until just starting to brown. Remove to a wire rack and cool. To serve, arrange cookies in a single layer on a plate. Prepare Cardamom Sugar (below); dust over the cookies.

CARDAMOM SUGAR

INGREDIENTS

1   tablespoon powdered sugar
⅛   teaspoon ground cardamom

DIRECTIONS

In a small bowl, thoroughly mix the powdered sugar and cardamom. Transfer to a fine mesh sieve.

*See Note on page 67

TOASTED-PECAN NUT BALLS

A hint of almond and toasted pecans lend marvelous flavor to this butter-ball cookie. Buy packaged, already-chopped raw pecan pieces or chips; the nuts tend to be uniform in size and toast more evenly.

- Makes about 3½ dozen –

INGREDIENTS

	Extra powdered sugar for dusting (about 2 tablespoons)
1	cup chopped pecan meats (chips or pieces)
1	cup (2 sticks) unsalted butter, softened
¾	cup powdered sugar
2	teaspoons pure vanilla extract
¼	teaspoon pure almond extract
½	teaspoon salt
2	cups all-purpose flour

DIRECTIONS

Toast the nuts (see Note page 17). Set aside and cool to room temperature.

Preheat the oven to 325 degrees F.

In a large bowl and with a mixer on medium speed, cream the butter until smooth, about 30 seconds. Gradually add ¾ cup powdered sugar and then beat until very light and fluffy, 4 to 5 minutes. Beat in both extracts and salt. Reduce speed to low. Gradually add the flour, mixing in each addition just until incorporated. Stir in the nuts with a wooden spoon.

Use 1 rounded tablespoon of dough per cookie and shape into balls. Space about 2 inches apart on ungreased baking sheets.

Bake for 20 minutes or until the edges are lightly browned. Cool for 1 to 2 minutes on the baking sheet. Transfer to a wire rack and cool completely. Dust with extra powdered sugar dredged through a fine-mesh sieve.

BARS & SQUARES

You will find plenty variety here. Textures range from crisp to cake-like, soft, crunchy, soft and chewy, and chewy-gooey. Toppings include nuts, powdered sugar, sugary glaze, icing, meringue or crusty dough. Furthermore, cutting the cookie slab into either bars or squares is always an option. The shapes and yields of these recipes are suggestions; feel free to portion as you like.

For flourless options, see also *No-Bake Peanut Butter Oat Squares* (page 210) and *My Favorite Granola Bars* (page 212).

PUMPKIN PIE SQUARES

Skip the round pie! This is a dessert to be served on a plate with a fork. Cut it into squares or rectangles—as big or small as you like. Top servings with a dollop of whipped cream if desired.

- Makes about 12 servings -

INGREDIENTS

CRUST

1	cup all-purpose flour
½	cup dry old-fashioned rolled oats (not quick-cooking or instant)
½	cup firmly packed light-brown sugar
½	cup (1 stick) cold unsalted butter, cut into small pieces

INGREDIENTS

FILLING

¾	cup granulated sugar
1	teaspoon ground cinnamon
½	teaspoon ground ginger
¼	teaspoon ground cloves
¼	teaspoon salt
2	large eggs
2	cups pure canned pumpkin puree (not pumpkin pie filling mix, it contains spices and salt)
1	can (12 ounces) evaporated milk
½	cup pecans (halves and pieces)

DIRECTIONS

Preheat the oven to 350 degrees F.

Have a 13x9x2-inch ungreased pan standing by.

Place all the crust ingredients into the bowl of a food processor fitted with a metal blade. Process until crumbly, about 20 pulses. Pat crumbs into the pan to form an even layer. Bake for 15 minutes; set aside to cool slightly.

Meanwhile, in a large bowl, combine all the filling ingredients—except pecans. Beat with a mixer on low speed just until smoothly blended. Pour the mixture over the crust. Bake for 30 minutes.

Sprinkle with pecans. Continue baking until a knife inserted into the center comes out clean, 15 to 25 minutes more. Place the pan on a wire rack and cool completely.

Note: Store in the refrigerator loosely covered. Serve chilled.

AUTUMN APPLE SQUARES

Use fragrant and tender McIntosh apples for wonderful fruity flavor. If you have no apple pie spice on hand, make your own (see Note below). You may want to eat these soft squares with a fork. They have a fabulous flavor, especially if the spice mixture includes clove. The surprise ingredient is coconut.

- Makes about 20 squares –

INGREDIENTS

Extra butter to grease the pan

CRUST

1½	cups all-purpose flour
⅓	cup granulated sugar
½	cup (1 stick) unsalted butter, softened

INGREDIENTS

TOPPING

2	large baking apples—peeled, cored, and sliced
2	tablespoons lemon juice
⅓	cup granulated sugar
1	teaspoon apple pie spice
1	large egg, lightly beaten
⅓	cup evaporated milk
1	teaspoon pure vanilla extract
¾	cup chopped pecans or walnuts
1⅓	cups sweetened flaked coconut

DIRECTIONS

Preheat the oven to 375 degrees F.

Lightly grease a 13x9x2-inch pan. Set aside.

In a large bowl, combine all crust ingredients. Beat with a mixer on low speed until fine crumbs form. Press the crumbs into the prepared pan. Arrange apple slices on top. Sprinkle with lemon juice. In a small bowl, combine ⅓ cup sugar and the spice; sprinkle evenly over the apples. Bake for 20 minutes.

Meanwhile, in a medium bowl, whisk together the egg, milk, and extract. Stir in the nuts and coconut. Spoon over the baked apples. Bake for 20 minutes more. Cool completely and cut into squares.

Note: TO MAKE APPLE PIE SPICE, combine 1½ teaspoons ground cinnamon, ¾ teaspoon ground nutmeg, ½ teaspoon ground all-spice, and ¼ teaspoon ground cloves or cardamom.

Note: Store apple squares in the refrigerator.

STRAWBERRY CHEESECAKE SQUARES

The crust is made with powdered sugar and melts in your mouth. The topping is a creamy cheesecake swirled with crushed strawberries in light syrup. Years ago, this recipe used frozen strawberries from a 10 ounce, box-like container—not gettable anymore. Today, bottled strawberries work beautifully here.

- Makes about 24 squares -

INGREDIENTS

CRUST

2	cups all-purpose flour
½	cup powdered sugar
⅔	cup cold unsalted butter, cut into small pieces

TOPPING

1	jar (10 ounces) whole strawberries in light syrup, undrained
2	packages (8 ounces each) cream cheese, softened
½	cup granulated sugar
2	large eggs

DIRECTIONS

Preheat the oven to 350 degrees F.

Have a 13x9x2-inch ungreased pan standing by.

Place all crust ingredients into a large bowl. Use a pastry blender to cut the butter into the dry ingredients until very fine crumbs form (or use a food processor to pulse the mixture). Press the crumbs into the pan to form an even layer. Bake for 15 minutes. Cool on a wire rack.

Meanwhile, place strawberries and their liquid into a 1-quart bowl. Use a fork or potato masher to mash the berries until very juicy and pulpy. Set aside.

In a medium bowl and with a mixer on low speed, beat the cream cheese until smooth and fluffy. Beat in the granulated sugar; beat in the eggs one at a time. Use a rubber spatula to stir in the mashed berries. Spread the mixture evenly over the cooled crust.

Bake for about 25 minutes or until the center is set. The top may puff up but will deflate upon cooling. Place the pan on a wire rack and cool completely. Chill until firm to cut, at least 4 hours.

> **Note:** Store in the refrigerator loosely covered. Serve chilled.

MAPLE WALNUT BARS

Strongly aromatic, I've used rum extract instead of maple and the bars are still wonderful.

- Makes about 36 bars –

INGREDIENTS

Extra butter to grease the pan

CRUST

1½ cups all-purpose flour

¼ cup firmly packed light-brown sugar

½ cup (1 stick) unsalted butter, softened

FILLING

¾ cup granulated sugar

2 tablespoons all-purpose flour

½ cup 100% pure maple syrup

2 tablespoons unsalted butter, melted

1 teaspoon maple extract

3 large eggs

1½ cups chopped walnuts

DIRECTIONS

Preheat the oven to 350 degrees F.

Lightly grease a 13x9x2-inch pan. Set aside.

Place all crust ingredients into a large bowl. Beat with a mixer on low speed until crumbly. Press crumbs into the prepared pan. Bake for 12 to 14 minutes or until lightly browned. Cool slightly.

Meanwhile, combine filling ingredients—except nuts—in a large bowl. Beat until blended; stir in nuts. Pour the filling over the warm crust. Continue to bake 20 to 30 minutes more or until the filling is set. Cool completely. Drizzle with Maple Glaze (below) and let it set. Cut into about 2x1½-inch bars.

MAPLE GLAZE

INGREDIENTS

1   cup powdered sugar
½   teaspoon maple extract
1 to 2   tablespoons milk (whole tastes best)

DIRECTIONS

Put powdered sugar and extract into a small bowl. Stir in enough milk to reach a desired consistency.

Note: Store refrigerated.

117

MAPLE PECAN SQUARES

A lovely combination of maple's complex sweetness and the fatty-rich taste of pecans come together in this cookie square. A buttery short-bread crust adds to the overall flavor. Store and serve the squares chilled to manage stickiness—if you must—because the flavor is just out-standing.

- Makes about 30 squares -

INGREDIENTS

Extra butter to grease the pan

CRUST

2   cups all-purpose flour
3   tablespoons granulated sugar
¼   teaspoon salt
¾   cup (1½ sticks) unsalted butter cut into 12 table-spoons, softened

TOPPING

¾   cup 100% pure maple syrup
¾   cup firmly packed light-brown sugar
2   large eggs
2   tablespoons unsalted butter, melted
¾   teaspoon pure vanilla extract
2   cups chopped pecans

DIRECTIONS

Preheat the oven to 350 degrees F.

Lightly grease a 13x9x1-inch jelly-roll pan. Set aside.

Put flour, granulated sugar, and salt into the bowl of a food processor fitted with a metal blade. Pulse to combine. Add ¾ cup butter; pulse until the mixture begins to clump. Press the dough into the prepared pan to form an even layer. Bake for 20 to 25 minutes or until lightly browned. Set aside to cool slightly.

Meanwhile, in a medium bowl, whisk together the topping ingredients—except pecans—until the brown sugar dissolves. Sprinkle pecans over the baked crust; evenly pour the syrup mixture over the top.

Return pan to the oven and bake for 20 to 25 minutes more or until the filling is set. Place the pan on a wire rack and cool completely. Cut into about 2-inch squares.

Note: Store refrigerated.

HAZELNUT SQUARES

Chopped roasted hazelnuts spiked with cinnamon are sprinkled over a buttery cardamom cookie base. This produces a sophisticated bite-size square, perfect to accompany a cup of hot coffee or black tea.

- Makes about 60 squares –

INGREDIENTS

	Extra butter to grease the pan
2	cups all-purpose flour
½	teaspoon ground cardamom
1	cup chopped roasted unsalted hazelnuts (filberts)
1	teaspoon ground cinnamon
3	tablespoons granulated sugar—plus 1 cup, divided use
1	cup (2 sticks) unsalted butter, softened
1	large egg, separated

DIRECTIONS

Preheat the oven to 300 degrees F.

Lightly grease a 15x10x1-inch jelly-roll pan. Set aside.

In a medium bowl, thoroughly whisk together the flour and cardamom. Set aside.

In a small bowl, toss nuts with the cinnamon and 3 tablespoons sugar. Set aside.

In a large bowl and with a mixer on medium speed, cream the butter until smooth, about 30 seconds. Gradually add the remaining 1 cup sugar; beat until well blended. Beat in the egg yolk. Use a wooden spoon to stir in the flour mixture in 4 parts. Transfer dough to the prepared pan; evenly spread and press it from the center to the sides of the pan.

Beat the egg white until foamy and brush over the dough. Sprinkle with the nut mixture. Lightly pat the top with fingertips to press nuts into the surface.

Bake for 1 hour. Cut into about 1½-inch squares while still hot. Cool in the pan for 20 to 30 minutes. While still warm, lift out squares with a spatula and place on a wire rack. Cool completely.

BLACK RASPBERRY JAM SQUARES

You can make these squares with red raspberry or strawberry jam, but the dark-berry color of black raspberry offers an inviting contrast to the golden hue of the crust. Plus, black raspberries have a more interesting, complex-organic flavor. It's the egg yolks that add enhanced color to the base dough.

- Makes about 16 squares -

INGREDIENTS

	Extra butter to grease the pan
	Powdered sugar for dusting (about 1 teaspoon)
1	cup (2 sticks) unsalted butter, softened
1	cup granulated sugar
2	egg yolks from large eggs
2	cups all-purpose flour
1	cup chopped walnuts
½	cup seedless black raspberry jam

DIRECTIONS

Preheat the oven to 325 degrees F.

Lightly grease a 9-inch square pan. Set aside.

In a large bowl and with a mixer on medium speed, cream the butter until smooth, about 30 seconds. Gradually add the sugar; beat until well blended. Beat in the egg yolks. Reduce speed to low.

Gradually beat in as much flour as you can with the mixer; stir in remaining flour with a wooden spoon. Stir in the nuts.

Gather the dough into a ball and cut it in half. Between the palms of your hands, pat one half into a square; place it in the center of the prepared pan. Spread dough to the edges of the pan, using slightly moistened fingertips if the dough seems sticky. Spread jam evenly over the dough. Pat remaining dough into another square and lay over the jam; spread and pat until it meets the edges of the pan.

Bake for 45 to 55 minutes or until golden brown. Place the pan on a wire rack. Cut into squares while still warm. Dust with powdered sugar dredged through a fine-mesh sieve.

Note: JAMS VS. PRESERVES: Use jam in this recipe. Preserves typically contain chunks of fruit. Jams are made from fruit pulp and have a more consistent thick mouth-feel; they're the perfect filling to spread between layers of dough.

SUNSHINE LEMON SQUARES

One large lemon will supply all the juice you'll need for this recipe; but, if unsure, buy two. Always choose a lemon that feels heavy for its size and gives a little when squeezed. It will yield more juice if it's at room temperature. This recipe easily doubles to make a 13x9x2-inch pan of luscious squares.

- Makes about 12 squares –

INGREDIENTS

CRUST

1   cup all-purpose flour
¼   cup powdered sugar
½   cup (1 stick) unsalted butter, softened

FILLING

2   large eggs
1   cup granulated sugar
2   tablespoons all-purpose flour
½   teaspoon baking powder
2   tablespoons fresh lemon juice

DIRECTIONS

Preheat the oven to 350 degrees F.

Have an 8-inch square ungreased pan standing by.

In a large bowl and with a mixer on low speed, beat all the crust ingredients until crumbly. Use lightly floured fingertips to pat crumbs into the pan. Bake for 20 minutes or until golden brown. Cool slightly.

Meanwhile, in a large bowl, combine the filling ingredients—except lemon juice. Beat until just blended. Stir in 2 tablespoons lemon juice.

Pour the filling over the warm crust. Bake an additional 25 minutes. Place the pan on a wire rack and cool completely. Spoon Lemon Glaze (below) evenly over the surface and let set. Cut into squares.

LEMON GLAZE

INGREDIENTS

½   cup powdered sugar
    About 1½ tablespoons fresh lemon juice

DIRECTIONS

In a small bowl, combine ½ cup powdered sugar and enough lemon juice to reach a desired consistency.

LEMON NUT SQUARES

A pecan-crumb mixture serves as both a crust and topping, enveloping a lemony cream-cheese filling.

- Makes about 24 squares -

INGREDIENTS

Extra butter to grease the pan

CRUST & TOPPING

1⅓   cups all-purpose flour

½   cup firmly packed light-brown sugar

¼   cup granulated sugar

¾   cup (1½ sticks) cold unsalted butter, cut into pieces

1   cup dry quick-cooking rolled oats (not instant or old-fashioned)

½   cup chopped pecans

INGREDIENTS

FILLING

1	package (8 ounces) cream cheese, softened
1	large egg
3	tablespoons fresh lemon juice
	Shaved zest from 2 large lemons*

DIRECTIONS

Preheat the oven to 350 degrees F.

Lightly grease a 13x9x2-inch pan. Set aside.

Place the flour, brown sugar, and granulated sugar into the bowl of a food processor fitted with a metal blade. Sprinkle butter pieces on top. Pulse until crumbs form. Transfer the mixture to a large bowl; stir in the oats and nuts. Reserve 1 cup. Press the remaining crumbs into the prepared pan to form an even layer. Bake for 15 minutes; set aside to cool slightly.

Meanwhile, in a medium bowl and with a mixer on low speed, beat the cream cheese until smooth. Beat in the egg, juice, and zest until blended. Scrape the mixture on top of the partially baked crust; spread evenly. Sprinkle with reserved crumbs. Return pan to the oven and bake for 25 minutes more.

Place the pan on a wire rack and cool completely. Cut into squares.

Note: Store in the refrigerator loosely covered. Serve chilled.

---

*See **Orange & Lemon Zest** (page XIII).

CHEWY FRUIT BARS

Use any combination of diced dried fruits, such as apricots, cranberries, cherries, dates, prunes, or whole raisins. The recipe easily doubles to make a generous 13x9x2-inch pan of soft and chewy bars. If desired, include walnuts to add crunchiness, too.

- Makes about 20 bars –

INGREDIENTS

	Cooking spray
	Powdered sugar for dusting (about 1 teaspoon)
1	cup all-purpose flour—plus 1 teaspoon, divided use
1	teaspoon baking powder
½	cup firmly packed light-brown sugar
4	tablespoons (½ stick) unsalted butter, melted
2	tablespoons orange juice
½	teaspoon pure vanilla extract
1	large egg
⅔	cup diced dried fruit or raisins (I love diced dates)
⅓	cup chopped walnuts (optional)

DIRECTIONS

Preheat the oven to 350 degrees F.

Lightly coat an 8-inch square pan with cooking spray. Set aside.

Into a 1-quart bowl, sift 1 cup flour with the baking powder; whisk briefly. Set aside.

In a large bowl, whisk together the brown sugar, melted butter, juice, extract, and egg. Use a rubber spatula to stir in the flour mixture just until almost incorporated. Put dried fruit (and nuts, if using) into a small bowl and toss with the remaining 1 teaspoon flour; fold into the batter. Scrape batter into the prepared pan; spread evenly.

Bake for 20 to 25 minutes or until a toothpick inserted into the center comes out clean. Place the pan on a wire rack and cool completely. Cut into about 2x1½-inch bars. Lightly dust with powdered sugar dredged through a fine-mesh sieve.

CHOCOLATE PEANUT BUTTER FINGERS

Better than a candy bar, these bars are truly finger-licking good. You really must make this recipe to know how special it is.

- Makes about 36 bars -

INGREDIENTS

½   cup (1 stick) unsalted butter, softened

½   cup granulated sugar

½   cup firmly packed light-brown sugar

1   large egg

⅓   cup creamy peanut butter

½   teaspoon pure vanilla extract

½   teaspoon baking soda

1   cup all-purpose flour

1   cup dry quick-cooking rolled oats (not instant or old-fashioned)

1   cup semisweet chocolate chips

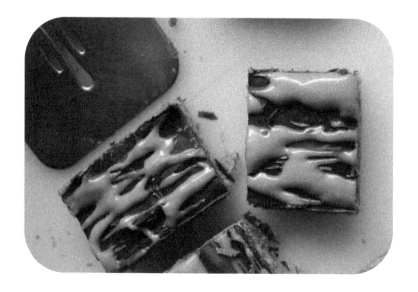

DIRECTIONS

Preheat the oven to 350 degrees F.

Have a 13x9x2-inch ungreased pan standing by.

In a large bowl and with a mixer on medium speed, cream the butter. Gradually add both sugars; beat until well blended. Beat in the egg, ⅓ cup peanut butter, extract, and baking soda. Use a wooden spoon to stir in the flour in 2 or 3 parts. Stir in the oats. Evenly press the mixture into the pan using a spatula lightly coated with cooking spray and/or moistened fingertips.

Bake for 20 minutes. Remove from the oven and immediately sprinkle with chocolate chips. Let stand until the chips are soft (about 5 minutes); spread evenly. Place the pan on a wire rack; cool completely. Drizzle with Peanut Butter Icing (below). Cut into about 2x1½-inch bars.

PEANUT BUTTER ICING

INGREDIENTS

¼	cup creamy peanut butter
½	cup powdered sugar
2 to 4	tablespoons evaporated milk

DIRECTIONS

In a 1-quart bowl and with a wooden spoon, cream the peanut butter with the powdered sugar. Vigorously stir in enough evaporated milk to reach a desired consistency.

PECAN TURTLE TRIANGLES

A cross between a cookie and a confection, this is an outstanding recipe. Originally, it made bars; the triangle shape is my contribution. A triangle enhances eating pleasure, encouraging smaller bites to be savored— try it and see for yourself. Plus, the pointed shape visually invites an initial bite.

- Makes about 6 dozen triangles –

INGREDIENTS

½   cup (1 stick) unsalted butter, softened—plus ¾ cup (1½ sticks), divided use

1   cup firmly packed light-brown sugar—plus ¾ cup, divided use

2   cups all-purpose flour

2½   cups pecan halves

2   cups milk-chocolate chips

½   cup chopped pecans

DIRECTIONS

Preheat the oven to 350 degrees F.

Have a 13x9x1-inch ungreased jelly-roll pan standing by.

In a large bowl, combine 1 stick softened butter, 1 cup brown sugar, and the flour. Beat with a mixer on low speed until fine crumbs form, 2 to 3 minutes. Lightly and evenly pat the crumbs into the pan.

Arrange 2½ cups pecan halves in a single layer over the top. Set aside.

In a 2-quart sauce pan, melt the remaining 1½ sticks butter with the remaining ¾ cup brown sugar. Cook over medium heat stirring constantly, 2 to 3 minutes, until the surface boils for about 1 minute. Immediately pour the mixture evenly over the nuts and crust.

Bake for 18 to 22 minutes or until the entire surface is bubbly and the crust is lightly browned. Remove from the oven and immediately sprinkle with chocolate chips. Let stand until the chips are soft (about 5 minutes); spread evenly. Sprinkle with ½ cup chopped pecans. Cool completely on a wire rack.

Run a thin knife blade around the edges of the pan to loosen the slab; cut it in half. Use a wide spatula to lift halves out of the pan and place on a large cutting surface. Cut into about 2x1½-inch rectangles, then cut each diagonally into triangles.

THE REAL DEAL
CHOCOLATE BROWNIES

This recipe produces a superb moist brownie. It offers the genuine, full-fatty flavor of 100% cacao chocolate and leaves a sweet-clean aftertaste. Be sure to carefully melt the chocolate with the butter. Some stoves have a special burner for melting chocolate, but you can use a regular burner on its lowest setting. Just stir constantly and—if needed—lift the pan off the heat occasionally to ensure slow melting.

- Makes about 24 brownies -

INGREDIENTS

	Extra butter to grease the pan
1	baking bar (4 ounces) unsweetened 100% cacao chocolate, coarsely chopped
½	cup (1 stick) unsalted butter
2	cups granulated sugar
4	large eggs
2	teaspoons pure vanilla extract
1	cup all-purpose flour
1	cup coarsely chopped walnuts

DIRECTIONS

Have all ingredients at room temperature.

Lightly grease a 13x9x2-inch pan (or see Note page 149). Set aside.

Put the chocolate and butter into a heavy 4-quart saucepan; place over very low heat. Stir constantly until the mixture is melted and smoothly blended. Set aside and cool completely to room temperature.

Preheat the oven to 350 degrees F.

Use a wooden spoon to stir the sugar into the chocolate-butter mixture. Thoroughly stir in the eggs one at a time, scraping sides of the pan with a rubber spatula as needed. Stir in the extract. Stir in the flour just until incorporated. Stir in the nuts. Scrape batter into the prepared pan; spread evenly.

Bake for 28 to 30 minutes or until the center is nearly firm when pressed with a fingertip and a toothpick inserted into the center comes out clean but slightly moist at the bottom. Place the pan on a wire rack and cool completely. Cut into about 2-inch squares.

> **Note:** Store squares loosely covered between layers of wax paper, and hold at a cool room temperature.

CHOCOLATE REVEL BARS

This recipe dates back to the early 1970's. Back then, a major ingredient—sweetened condensed milk— came in 15-ounce cans; today 14 ounces is the norm. The recipe still works beautifully. These bars are so deeply rich and chocolaty—they are truly extraordinary.

- Makes about 50 bars –

INGREDIENTS

CRUST & TOPPPING

2½ cups all-purpose flour

1 teaspoon baking soda

½ teaspoon salt

3 cups dry quick-cooking rolled oats (not instant or old-fashioned)

1 cup (2 sticks) unsalted butter, softened

2 cups firmly packed light-brown sugar

2 large eggs

2 teaspoons pure vanilla extract

CHOCOLATE LAYER

1 can (14 ounces) sweetened condensed milk

2 cups semisweet chocolate chips

2 tablespoons unsalted butter

2 teaspoons pure vanilla extract

1 cup chopped walnuts

DIRECTIONS

Preheat the oven to 350 degrees F.

Have a 15x10x1-inch ungreased jelly-roll pan standing by.

PREPARE CRUST & TOPPING:

Into a large bowl, sift the flour with the baking soda and salt. Thoroughly stir in the oats. Set aside. In another large bowl and with a mixer on medium speed, cream 1 cup butter. Gradually beat in the brown sugar. Beat in the eggs one at a time; beat in 2 teaspoons extract. Use a wooden spoon to gradually stir in the flour mixture. Reserve ⅓ of the dough. Evenly press ⅔ dough into the pan.

PREPARE CHOCOLATE LAYER:

In a 3-quart saucepan, combine milk, chocolate, and 2 tablespoons butter. Place over low heat; stir until blended. Stir in 2 teaspoons extract and nuts. Spread mixture over the dough; dot with reserved dough.

Bake for 30 minutes. Cool completely. Cut into about 3x2-inch bars, and then cut each bar into halves.

MAGIC COOKIE BARS

Here's a popular-magazine recipe from bygone years. Use whatever type of nuts you have on hand. Coarsely chopped walnuts give the bars a deluxe appearance and texture; pecans add rich flavor; hazelnuts and even peanuts work out well.

- Makes about 36 bars -

INGREDIENTS

½   cup (1 stick) margarine or butter

1½   cups crushed graham cracker crumbs (about 18 squares crushed—see Note page 19)

1   can (14 ounces) sweetened condensed milk

2   cups semisweet chocolate chips

1¼   cups sweetened flaked coconut

1   cup chopped nuts (your choice, pecans are my preference)

DIRECTIONS

Preheat the oven to 350 degrees F.
Have a 13x9x2-inch ungreased pan standing by.

Put the margarine or butter into the pan; place in the hot oven and heat until just melted. Remove the pan and sprinkle crumbs evenly over the top. Pour sweetened condensed milk evenly over the crumbs. Evenly layer with remaining ingredients, pressing down gently.

Return pan to the oven and bake for 25 minutes or until lightly browned. Place on a wire rack and cool completely. Cut into about 2x1½-inch bars.

CHOCOLATE NUT SQUARES

This is a cookie confection comprised of a crunchy, chocolate-coconut topping and a shortbread crust. The recipe is from a 1990's advertisement for a well-known margarine. Substituting butter produces a brittle texture, so use margarine. Cut the slab as you like, however squares—about 2x2 inch—suit well.

- Makes about 16 squares –

INGREDIENTS

CRUST

½	cup (1 stick) margarine, cut into about 8 pieces
¼	cup granulated sugar
1¼	cups all-purpose flour

TOPPING

4	tablespoons (½ stick) margarine
½	cup granulated sugar
2	tablespoons heavy cream
1¾	cups chopped walnuts or pecans
1	cup sweetened flaked coconut
¾	cup semisweet chocolate chips

DIRECTIONS

Preheat the oven to 350 degrees F.

Have a 9-inch square ungreased pan standing by.

In a large bowl, combine all crust ingredients. Beat with a mixer on low speed until fine crumbs form. Evenly press the crumbs into the pan. Bake for 18 to 20 minutes or until the edges are lightly browned.

Meanwhile, in a 3-quart saucepan, combine 4 tablespoons margarine, ½ cup sugar, and the cream. Gently heat and stir until the margarine melts and the mixture is blended. Stir in the nuts.

Sprinkle coconut and chocolate chips over the hot crust. Evenly spread the nut mixture on top. Return the pan to the oven and bake for 20 minutes more. Place on a wire rack and cool completely. Run a thin metal spatula around the edges of the pan to loosen the slab. Cut into squares or bars.

NUTTY CHOCOLATE
MERINGUE SQUARES

Use coarsely chopped pecans, walnuts, whole dry-roasted peanuts or salted peanuts—whatever you like. If desired, double the recipe and use a 13x9x2-inch pan.

- Makes about 12 squares -

INGREDIENTS

   Extra butter to grease the pan

1   cup all-purpose flour

½   teaspoon baking soda

¼   teaspoon salt

4   tablespoons (½ stick) unsalted butter, softened

¼   cup granulated sugar

¼   cup firmly packed light-brown sugar—plus ½ cup, divided use

1   large egg, separated

½   teaspoon pure vanilla extract

½   cup semisweet chocolate chips

¼   to ½ cup nut meats or whole peanuts (I like salted peanuts)

DIRECTIONS

Preheat the oven to 325 degrees F.

Lightly grease an 8-inch square pan. Set aside.

Into a medium bowl, sift together the flour, baking soda, and salt; whisk briefly. Set aside.

In a large bowl and with a mixer on medium speed, cream the butter. Gradually add the granulated sugar and ¼ cup brown sugar; beat until well blended. Beat in the egg yolk and extract. Use a wooden spoon to gradually stir in the flour mixture, blending until crumbs form.

Evenly press the crumbs into the prepared pan. Sprinkle chocolate chips and nuts over the surface.

With clean beaters and in a 1-quart bowl, beat the egg white until foamy and slightly mounded. Gradually beat in the remaining ½ cup brown sugar, and then beat until very stiff peaks form. Spread over the chocolate chips and nuts.

Bake for 35 minutes. Place the pan on a wire rack to cool. Cut into squares while still warm.

Note: These are best eaten the day they're made. Store leftovers tightly covered with foil and hold at room temperature.

MOCHA-ALMOND BARS

These bars are for the mature palate. Espresso powder adds a sophisticated, borderline-bitter flavor, and roughly chopped almonds crown the top with crunchy texture—DELICIOUS.

- Makes about 25 bars –

INGREDIENTS

2	cups all-purpose flour
2	teaspoons instant espresso powder
¼	teaspoon salt
1	cup (2 sticks) unsalted butter, softened
1	cup firmly packed light-brown sugar
1	large egg, separated
1	teaspoon pure almond extract
½	teaspoon pure vanilla extract
1	cup semisweet chocolate chips
¾	cup coarsely chopped almonds

DIRECTIONS

Preheat the oven to 350 degrees F.

Have a 15x10x1-inch ungreased jelly-roll pan standing by.

Into a medium bowl, sift the flour with the espresso powder and salt; whisk briefly. Set aside.

In a large bowl and with a mixer on medium speed, cream the butter until smooth, about 30 seconds. Gradually add the brown sugar and then beat until very well blended. Beat in the egg yolk and extracts. Reduce speed to low. Gradually beat in as much flour mixture as you can with the mixer; stir in remaining flour with a wooden spoon. Stir in the chocolate chips.

Scrape the dough into the pan; evenly spread it from the center to the edges. (If the dough is sticky, use a rubber spatula coated with cooking spray.) Beat the egg white until foamy and brush over the dough. Sprinkle nuts on top; gently pat them into the surface.

Bake for 20 minutes. Place the pan on a wire rack and cool completely. Cut into about 3x2-inch bars.

CHOCOLATE-CHIP COOKIE BARS

Here's a relaxed, fun alternative to chocolate chip cookies. The ingredients for these bars could be in your pantry right now. Mini chips work especially well in this recipe, but regular chips are good, too.

- Makes about 24 bars -

INGREDIENTS

Extra butter to grease the pan

2	cups all-purpose flour
1	teaspoon baking powder
½	teaspoon salt
1	cup (2 sticks) unsalted butter, softened
1	cup granulated sugar
1	teaspoon pure vanilla extract
⅔	cup mini-semisweet chocolate chips (or 1 cup regular chips)
½	cup chopped walnuts or pecans

DIRECTIONS

Preheat the oven to 350 degrees F.

Lightly grease a 13x9x1-inch jelly-roll pan. Set aside.

Into a medium bowl, sift the flour with the baking powder and salt; whisk briefly. Set aside.

In a large bowl and with a mixer on medium speed, cream the butter until smooth, about 30 seconds. Gradually add the sugar and then beat until very well combined. Beat in the extract. Use a wooden spoon to gradually stir in the flour mixture. Blend in the chips and nuts. Evenly press the dough into the prepared pan.

Bake for about 35 minutes. Cut into bars while still very warm. Continue to cool in the pan until firm enough to remove (the bars should still be warm). Place bars on a wire rack and cool completely.

CHOCOLATE-CHIP BARS WITH BANANA

This goody makes a wonderful snack-cake; the baked slab slices into sturdy, cake-like portions.

– Makes about 32 bars –

INGREDIENTS

Aluminum foil (see Note below)

Extra butter to lightly grease the foil

1 cup (2 sticks) unsalted butter, softened

1 cup granulated sugar

1 cup firmly packed dark-brown sugar

3 large eggs

½ teaspoon salt

1 medium very ripe banana, mashed

2 teaspoons pure vanilla extract

3 cups all-purpose flour

1 cup chocolate chips

1 cup coarsely chopped walnuts or pecans

DIRECTIONS

Preheat the oven to 350 degrees F.

Line a 13x9x2-inch pan with foil, allowing it to overhang the two narrow ends of the pan by 2 inches. Lightly grease the foil. Set aside.

In a large bowl and with a mixer on medium speed, cream the butter until smooth, about 30 seconds. Gradually add both sugars; beat until blended, about 3 minutes. Beat in the eggs one at a time. Beat in the salt, banana, and extract. Reduce speed to low. Gradually beat in the flour. Stir in chips and nuts. Scrape dough into the prepared pan; spread evenly.

Bake for 35 to 40 minutes or until a toothpick inserted into the center comes out clean. Place on a wire rack and cool completely. Use foil overhang to lift the slab out of the pan and place it on a cutting surface. Cut into bars or squares, as you like. Alternatively, leave in the pan and cut as you snack.

> **Note: NON-STICK HEAVY DUTY ALUMINUM FOIL** works beautifully here and for most bars or squares that require a greased pan. (Use dull side up, facing food.) To fit foil to the pan, turn upside down and smooth foil to its shape. Turn pan over and smooth foil inside, leaving an overhang. When cool, use the overhang to lift the slab out of the pan. If desired, trim away the dry edges. **If using ordinary foil (not non-stick), lightly grease it.**

FANCY COOKIES

When you want to make a special impression, here's a collection of cookies that are a little more fussed over. The effort is worth it; each one is a gem—attractive as well as delicious.

SOUR CREAM DROPS WITH COCONUT FROSTING

These cookies taste as delectable as they look.

- Makes about 4 dozen -

INGREDIENTS

Extra butter to grease the baking sheets

1½ cups all-purpose flour, plus 2 tablespoons

1½ teaspoons baking powder

½ teaspoon baking soda

½ teaspoon salt

½ cup (1 stick) unsalted butter, softened

¾ cup firmly packed light-brown sugar

1 large egg

1 yolk from a large egg

½ cup sour cream

½ teaspoon pure vanilla extract

½ cup chopped pecans

DIRECTIONS

Preheat the oven to 375 degrees F.

Lightly grease baking sheets. Set aside.

Into a medium bowl, sift together the first 4 dry ingredients (flour through salt); whisk briefly. Set aside.

In a large bowl and with a mixer on medium speed, cream the butter. Gradually add the brown sugar; beat until fluffy. Beat in the egg, yolk, sour cream, and extract. Reduce speed to low. Add the flour mixture in 3 parts; beat just until each addition is incorporated. Use a wooden spoon to stir in the nuts.

Drop dough by level tablespoons onto the prepared baking sheets, spacing about 2 inches apart.

Bake for 12 minutes. Cool cookies on the sheet for 1 minute. Transfer to a wire rack and cool completely. Spread tops with Coconut Frosting (below) and sprinkle with flaked coconut.

COCONUT FROSTING

INGREDIENTS

1	cup powdered sugar
2	tablespoons unsalted butter, softened
½	teaspoon pure vanilla extract
1	tablespoon whole milk
1	cup sweetened flaked coconut, for sprinkling

DIRECTIONS

Put powdered sugar, butter, and extract into a medium bowl. Add 1 tablespoon milk and beat with a mixer until smooth. If needed, add additional drops of milk to reach a desired consistency.

THUMBPRINT COOKIES

Usually filled with jelly or fruit preserves, thumbprints are just so pretty when filled with tinted icing. Use pastel tints for springtime or a baby shower; use bright red and green for Christmas; or a bold green for St. Patrick's Day. If desired, fill the cookies with preserves, jam or jelly instead of icing.

- Makes about 3 dozen –

INGREDIENTS

4	tablespoons (½ stick) unsalted butter, softened
4	tablespoons shortening, at room temperature
¼	cup firmly packed light-brown sugar

1	large egg, separated
½	teaspoon pure vanilla extract
1	cup all-purpose flour
1	to 1¼ cups finely chopped pecans

DIRECTIONS

Preheat the oven to 350 degrees F.

In a large bowl and with a mixer on medium speed, cream the butter and shortening until smoothly blended. Add the brown sugar and beat until very well combined. Beat in the egg yolk and extract. Reduce speed to low. Add the flour in about 4 parts, mixing just until each addition is incorporated.

Put nuts into a small bowl. Lightly beat the egg white in another small bowl. Shape level ½ tablespoons of dough into balls. Dip each ball into egg white and then roll in nuts to cover allover. Place 2 inches apart on ungreased baking sheets. Press your thumb deeply into the center of each ball to form a well.

Bake for 10 minutes or until lightly browned. (If the wells inflated during baking, press your thumb back into the spot while the cookies are still warm on the baking sheet.) Transfer cookies to a wire rack when firm enough to move. Cool completely. Fill the wells with Tinted Icing (below).

TINTED ICING

INGREDIENTS

1	cup powdered sugar
1	tablespoon heavy cream
	Food coloring

DIRECTIONS

In a 1-quart bowl and with a wooden spoon, beat the powdered sugar with 1 tablespoon cream. Beat in additional small amounts of cream until a desired consistency is reached. Stir in drops of food coloring.

CHOCOLATE-DIPPED COCONUT MACAROONS

Macaroons were invented in Italy but became popular in France. In the 18th century, it was a custom in many French convents for the nuns to bake macaroons. Ingredients included just egg whites, sugar and almond paste. Today, there are many variations of macaroon recipes. Below, is one that uses flour, sweetened condensed milk and no eggs. It produces a very rich and chewy cookie.

- Makes about 2 dozen -

INGREDIENTS

Parchment paper

1	package (7 ounces) sweetened flaked coconut (about 2½ cups)
⅓	cup all-purpose flour
⅛	teaspoon salt
⅔	cup sweetened condensed milk
1	teaspoon pure vanilla extract
4	ounces dark-bittersweet chocolate, melted

DIRECTIONS

Preheat the oven to 350 degrees F.

Line 2 baking sheets with parchment paper. Set aside.

In a large bowl, thoroughly toss together the coconut, flour, and salt. Stir in the milk and extract. Drop level tablespoons of the mixture onto the prepared baking sheets, spacing about 2 inches apart.

(For polished looking cookies, gently roll each mound of mixture between slightly dampened palms until just rounded and a bit smoothed.)

Bake each sheet separately for 15 to 17 minutes or until lightly browned. Transfer baking sheets to a wire rack and let the cookies cool completely on the sheet.

Dip the top of each cookie into melted chocolate; place on a jelly-roll pan and let the chocolate set. Briefly place the pan in the freezer to firm the chocolate, about 5 minutes.

> **Note:** For the dark chocolate, use a 4-ounce Ghirardelli bittersweet 60% cocoa premium baking bar.

> **Note:** Store macaroons in an airtight container between layers of saran or wax paper. Hold in the refrigerator for up to one week. Return to room temperature before serving. Freeze for longer storage.

COCONUT–ALMOND BALLS

This not-too-sweet cookie is nicely complemented with a light dusting of powdered sugar or scant drizzle of melted semi-sweet chocolate. If preferred, the dough can be shaped into crescents or logs.

– Makes about 3 dozen –

INGREDIENTS

Extra granulated sugar to flatten cookies (about 2 tablespoons)

Powdered sugar for dusting (about 1 tablespoon)

About ⅓ cup semisweet chocolate chips, melted for drizzle

½   cup sliced almonds

½   cup sweetened flaked coconut

1   cup (2 sticks) unsalted butter, softened

½   cup granulated sugar

1   egg yolk from a large egg

¼   teaspoon salt

2½   cups all-purpose flour

DIRECTIONS

Preheat the oven to 350 degrees F.

In a food processor fitted with a metal blade, pulse the almonds and coconut until ground. Set aside.

In a large bowl and with a mixer on medium speed, cream the butter until smooth, about 30 seconds. Gradually add ½ cup granulated sugar and then beat until light and fluffy, 3 to 4 minutes. Beat in the egg yolk and salt. Use a wooden spoon to stir in the almond-coconut mixture; gradually stir in the flour.

Put the extra granulated sugar into a small bowl. Use 1 level tablespoon of dough per cookie and shape into balls. Space about 2 inches apart on ungreased baking sheets. Slightly flatten with the greased bottom of a drinking glass dipped into the extra sugar.

Bake for 10 to 12 minutes or until golden brown on the bottoms. Transfer cookies to a wire rack and cool completely. Dust with powdered sugar dredged through a fine-mesh sieve or drizzle with melted semisweet chocolate.

MOM'S MELTING MOMENTS

When you eat this cookie, every bite melts on your tongue—quickly, thanks to the addition of cornstarch. If desired, dust finished cookies lightly with extra powdered sugar to enhance sweetness. Sometimes, Mom added two teaspoons of orange or lemon zest along with the extract—feel free to do so, too.

- Makes about 33 cookies -

INGREDIENTS

About 1 generous cup of sweetened flaked coconut

1¾   cups all-purpose flour

¼   cup cornstarch

1   cup (2 sticks) unsalted butter, softened

½   cup powdered sugar

1   teaspoon pure vanilla extract

DIRECTIONS

Preheat the oven to 300 degrees F.

Into a medium bowl, sift together the flour and cornstarch; whisk briefly. Set aside.

In a large bowl and with a mixer on medium speed, cream the butter until smooth, about 30 seconds. Gradually add the powdered sugar and then beat until light and fluffy, about 4 minutes. Beat in the extract. Use a wooden spoon to gradually stir in the flour mixture.

Put the coconut into a shallow bowl. Use 1 level tablespoon of dough per cookie and shape into balls. Roll each ball in coconut to cover allover. Space about 2 inches apart on ungreased baking sheets. Flatten slightly with a floured fork if desired.

Bake 20 to 25 minutes or until lightly browned. Allow cookies to cool on the sheet until firm enough to move. Transfer to a wire rack and cool completely.

Note: The cookies are a bit delicate. Store them between layers of saran in an airtight container and hold in the freezer. They thaw in minutes.

PECAN SHORTBREAD COOKIES WITH VANILLA ICING

Butter pecan ice cream is what I think of when eating this cookie.
   For best results, use a good quality pure vanilla extract—here and always.

- Makes about 35 cookies –

INGREDIENTS

½   cup (1 stick) unsalted butter, softened

⅔   cup granulated sugar

1   large egg

½   teaspoon salt

2   teaspoons pure vanilla extract

2   cups all-purpose flour

1½   cups coarsely chopped pecans

162

DIRECTIONS

Preheat the oven to 325 degrees F.

In a large bowl and with a mixer on medium speed, cream the butter until smooth. Gradually add the sugar; beat until fluffy and well blended. Beat in the egg, salt, and extract. Use a wooden spoon to gradually stir in the flour. (The dough will be quite stiff.) Thoroughly blend in the nuts.

Drop dough by level tablespoons onto ungreased baking sheets, spacing about 2 inches apart. If desired, flatten with a fork for a less doughy-tasting cookie.

Bake for 13 to 14 minutes or until the bottoms are lightly browned (lift a cookie and check). Transfer to a wire rack and cool completely. Drizzle with Vanilla Icing (below).

VANILLA ICING

INGREDIENTS

1	cup powdered sugar
1	tablespoon milk (whole tastes best)
½	teaspoon pure vanilla extract

DIRECTIONS

In a 1-quart bowl and with a wooden spoon, stir together all the ingredients. Add additional drops of milk to reach a desired consistency. Use immediately.

> **Note:** Dark, non-stick baking sheets are recommended; these cookies brown best on this type of surface.

VIENNESE REFRIGERATOR COOKIES

This slice-and-bake refrigerator cookie dough freezes beautifully. Just form it into logs, wrap airtight and store in the freezer. When ready to bake, slice logs crosswise into rounds. The dough slices best when it's very cold or still quite frozen.

- Makes about 5 dozen -

INGREDIENTS

	Saran or wax paper
	Apricot and/or seedless red raspberry preserves
	About ½ cup semisweet chocolate chips, melted for drizzle
¾	cup (1½ sticks) unsalted butter, softened
½	cup granulated sugar
1	large egg
½	cup ground pecans (see Note page 67)
2	cups all-purpose flour

DIRECTIONS

In a large bowl and with a mixer on medium speed, cream the butter until smooth. Gradually add the sugar and then beat until very well blended. Beat in the egg; beat in the ground nuts. Reduce speed to low. Gradually mix in the flour just until each addition is incorporated. Gather dough into a disk.

Divide dough in half. (If you have a kitchen scale, each half will weigh about 10.5 ounces.) Shape each half into a log approximately 10 inches long. Tightly wrap the logs separately in saran or wax paper.

Refrigerate overnight or place in a heavy zipper-top plastic bag and freeze for up to two months.

Preheat the oven to 350 degrees F.

Unwrap logs. Cut into ¼-inch-thick slices and place on ungreased sheets, spacing about 1 inch apart.

Bake for 13 to 15 minutes or until light golden brown. Promptly transfer cookies to a wire rack; cool completely. Spread a thin layer of preserves over each cookie. Drizzle lightly with melted chocolate. Chill cookies in the fridge to firm the chocolate or put them into the freezer for about 5 minutes.

> **Note:** Store cookies frozen in an airtight container between layers of saran. When ready to serve, remove the number of cookies desired. They will defrost in minutes and look perfectly beautiful.

ALMOND HALF-MOON REFRIGERATOR COOKIES

I've retooled this recipe to use almond flour instead of grinding the hard nuts; it works beautifully.

– Makes about 5 dozen –

INGREDIENTS

Saran or wax paper

Extra butter to grease the baking sheets

Extra granulated sugar for sprinkling

2½ cups all-purpose flour

½ cup raw almond flour

1 teaspoon baking powder

½ teaspoon salt

1 cup (2 sticks) unsalted butter, softened

1 cup granulated sugar

1 large egg

1 egg yolk from a large egg

1 teaspoon pure almond extract

1 egg white, lightly beaten

1 cup sliced almonds, roughly chopped

DIRECTIONS

Into a medium bowl, sift together both flours, baking powder, and salt; whisk briefly. Set aside.

In a large bowl and with a mixer on medium speed, cream the butter until smooth, about 30 seconds. Slowly add the sugar; beat 4 to 5 minutes. Beat in the egg, yolk, and extract. Reduce speed to low. Gradually add the flour mixture, beating in as much as you can with the mixer. Stir in remaining flour.

Gather dough into a disk; divide in half. (If you have a kitchen scale, each half will weigh about 15 ounces.) Shape each half into a log approximately 7 inches long and 2 inches in diameter. Tightly wrap the logs separately in saran or wax paper. Refrigerate overnight or freeze for up to two months.

Preheat the oven to 350 degrees F.

Lightly grease baking sheets. Set aside.

Unwrap logs. Cut into ¼-inch-thick rounds; cut rounds in half. Use fingertips to shape half-circles into a curved half-moon shape. Place on prepared baking sheets. Brush with egg white; sprinkle with nuts.

Bake for 10 minutes or until golden brown on the bottoms. Transfer cookies to a wire rack and sprinkle with a bit of extra granulated sugar. Cool Completely.

LEMON HEARTS

These cookies are sweetly tart and very pretty.

- Makes about 3 dozen -

INGREDIENTS

Parchment paper

1 cup (2 sticks) unsalted butter, softened

1 cup granulated sugar

½ teaspoon salt

1 large egg

1 egg yolk from a large egg

2 teaspoons pure vanilla extract

½ tablespoon shaved lemon zest *

2½ cups all-purpose flour

DIRECTIONS

In a large bowl and with a mixer on medium speed, cream the butter until smooth. Slowly add the sugar; beat 4 to 5 minutes. Beat in the salt, egg, yolk, extract, and zest. Reduce speed to low. Gradually mix in the flour. Divide dough in half; wrap each half in saran. Chill for at least 1 hour.

Preheat the oven to 375 degrees F.

Line baking sheets with parchment paper. Set aside.

On a floured surface, roll dough to a ⅛-inch thickness. Cut with a 3-inch heart-shaped cutter. Use a 1-inch cutter to cut out and remove centers. Transfer to the prepared baking sheets, spacing 1 inch apart.

Bake for 6 to 8 minutes or until golden brown. Transfer cookies to a wire rack to cool. Prepare Lemon Icing (below). Dip top side of cookies into the icing. Place on a rack and allow to dry for 30 minutes.

LEMON ICING

INGREDIENTS

1	cup powdered sugar
1	teaspoon shaved lemon zest*
	About 2 tablespoons fresh lemon juice

DIRECTIONS

Combine sugar and zest in a wide bowl. Stir in enough juice to reach a desired consistency.

*See **Orange & Lemon Zest** (page XIII).

LEMON BALLS

A scrumptious cookie, it's encrusted with toasted nuts and topped with a lemony frosting. The dough is made with corn starch and powdered sugar; it yields a tender crumb texture that melts in your mouth.

- Makes about 3 dozen –

INGREDIENTS

1½	cups blanched slivered almonds
1½	cups all-purpose flour
¾	cup cornstarch
½	teaspoon salt
1	cup (2 sticks) unsalted butter, softened
½	cup powdered sugar
	Shaved zest from 1 large lemon*

DIRECTIONS

Toast the nuts (see Note page 17). Cool completely and then finely chop. Set aside.

Preheat the oven to 350 degrees F.

Into a medium bowl, sift the flour with the cornstarch and salt; whisk briefly. Set aside.

In a large bowl and with a mixer on medium speed, cream the butter. Slowly add the powder sugar; beat for about 4 minutes. Beat in the zest. Reduce speed to low. Add the flour mixture in 4 parts.

Put nuts into a shallow bowl. Use 1 level tablespoon of dough per cookie and shape into balls. Roll in nuts, patting them in, to coat allover. Space about 2 inches apart on ungreased baking sheets.

Bake for 15 to 17 minutes or until lightly browned. Transfer cookies to a wire rack; cool completely. Spread the tops with Lemon Frosting (below) and let set.

LEMON FROSTING

INGREDIENTS

1   cup powdered sugar
2   tablespoons unsalted butter, melted
1   tablespoon fresh lemon juice

DIRECTIONS

In a medium bowl and with a wooden spoon, cream the ingredients together until smoothly blended.

*See **Orange & Lemon Zest** (page XIII).

RASPBERRY SHORTBREAD

Beautiful and fragrant, this is a luscious cookie with strong sensory appeal. The dough is constructed into strips, filled, baked and then cut into attractive diagonal slices.

- Makes about 6 dozen -

INGREDIENTS

1	cup (2 sticks) unsalted butter, softened
⅔	cup granulated sugar
2½	cups all-purpose flour
1	jar (10 ounces) seedless red raspberry jam

DIRECTIONS

Preheat the oven to 350 degrees F.

In a large bowl and with a mixer on medium speed, cream the butter. Slowly add the granulated sugar and then beat until light and fluffy, about 4 minutes. Reduce speed to low. Gradually beat in as much flour as you can with the mixer; use a wooden spoon to stir in remaining flour.

Divide dough into 6 equal parts. (If you have a kitchen scale, each portion will weigh about 4 ounces.) Roll each portion into a 12-inch log. Transfer to ungreased baking sheets and—with fingertips—flatten into strips 1-inch wide and ½-inch high. Use your index finger to make an indentation in each strip that is ½-inch wide and ¼-inch deep. Spoon half of jam into the indentations.

Bake for 15 minutes. Remove from the oven and spoon remaining jam into the indentations. Return pan to the oven and bake 5 minutes more or until lightly browned.

Prepare Almond Glaze (below) and drizzle it over the warm shortbread while still on the baking sheets. Put the sheets on wire racks to cool. Cut each shortbread strip diagonally into 1-inch slices.

ALMOND GLAZE

INGREDIENTS

1	cup powdered sugar
½	teaspoon pure almond extract
	About 1 tablespoon water

DIRECTIONS

Put the powdered sugar and extract into a 1-quart bowl. Stir in enough water to reach a smooth and desired consistency.

FROSTED SALTY CASHEW COOKIES

This is a superb cookie even without the frosting and cashew on top. For best flavor and browning, use lightly buttered shiny-metal baking sheets.

- Makes about 3½ dozen –

INGREDIENTS

Extra butter to grease the baking sheets

Extra whole cashews for garnish

2   cups all-purpose flour

¾   teaspoon baking powder

¾   teaspoon baking soda

¼   teaspoon salt

½   cup (1 stick) unsalted butter, softened

1   cup firmly packed light-brown sugar

1   large egg

½   teaspoon pure vanilla extract

⅓   cup sour cream

1¾ cups whole cashews with sea salt

DIRECTIONS

Preheat the oven to 400 degrees F.

Lightly grease baking sheets. Set aside.

Into a medium bowl, sift the first 4 dry ingredients (flour through salt); whisk briefly. Set aside.

In a large bowl and with a mixer on medium speed, cream the butter. Gradually add the brown sugar; beat until blended. Beat in the egg and extract. Reduce speed to low. Add the flour mixture alternating with sour cream, beginning and ending with the flour mixture. Stir in the nuts with a wooden spoon.

Drop dough by rounded tablespoons onto the prepared baking sheets, spacing about 2 inches apart.

Bake for about 10 minutes or until lightly browned. Transfer cookies to a wire rack; cool completely. Spread Brown Butter Frosting (below) on top of each cookie. Garnish with an extra whole cashew.

BROWN BUTTER FROSTING

INGREDIENTS

3	tablespoons unsalted butter
1	teaspoon pure vanilla extract
3	cups powdered sugar
3 to 4	tablespoons whole milk

DIRECTIONS

In a 3-quart saucepan, cook the butter until delicately browned. Remove from the heat. Stir in the extract and powdered sugar. Add enough milk to reach a desired consistency, beating vigorously.

TOASTED ALMOND DROPS

Here's a dainty cookie with powerful flavor. Dark-brown sugar gives the impression of butterscotch, and toasted-sliced almonds—sugared—contribute nutty flavor and sporadic crunchy texture.

- Makes about 4 dozen -

INGREDIENTS

½   cup sliced almonds

1   tablespoon granulated sugar

½   cup (1 stick) unsalted butter, softened

½   cup firmly packed dark-brown sugar

1   large egg

¼   teaspoon pure almond extract

1   cup all-purpose flour

DIRECTIONS

Preheat the oven to 375 degrees F.

Put the almonds into a small dry skillet and place on the stovetop over medium-low heat. Stir until slightly fragrant, about 1 minute. Sprinkle 1 tablespoon granulated sugar over the nuts and stir constantly until the sugar melts and the almonds become brown and toasted. Immediately transfer to a plate and cool completely. Break up clusters with your fingertips. Set aside.

In a large bowl and with a mixer on medium speed, cream the butter until smooth. Gradually add the brown sugar and then beat until well blended. Beat in the egg and extract. Reduce speed to low.

Gradually beat in as much flour as you can with the mixer. Use a wooden spoon to stir in remaining flour. Stir in the toasted-sugared nuts.

Drop level ½ tablespoons of dough onto ungreased baking sheets, spacing about 2 inches apart.

Bake for 8 to 10 minutes or until the bottoms are browned. Transfer cookies to a wire rack when firm enough to move, 1 to 2 minutes. Cool completely.

OATMEAL COOKIES WITH ESPRESSO FROSTING

A mature palate will appreciate this recipe. It uses nutmeg and coarsely chopped pecans instead of the usual cinnamon and walnuts. Espresso enhances the overall flavor and leaves a coffee-like aftertaste.

– Makes about 3 dozen –

INGREDIENTS

1 cup all-purpose flour

½ teaspoon baking soda

¼ teaspoon baking powder

¼ teaspoon salt

⅛ teaspoon ground nutmeg

½ cup (1 stick) unsalted butter, softened

½ cup firmly packed light-brown sugar

½ cup granulated sugar

1 large egg

1 teaspoon pure vanilla extract

1½ cups dry quick-cooking rolled oats (not instant or old-fashioned)

½ cup coarsely chopped pecans

DIRECTIONS

Preheat the oven to 350 degrees F.

Into a 1-quart bowl, sift the first 5 dry ingredients (flour through nutmeg); whisk briefly. Set aside.

In a large bowl and with a mixer on medium speed, cream the butter until smooth. Gradually add both sugars and then beat until very well blended. Beat in the egg and extract. Use a rubber spatula to stir in the flour mixture. Stir in the oats and nuts.

Drop dough by level tablespoons onto ungreased baking sheets, spacing about 2 inches apart.

Bake for 10 minutes or until lightly browned around the edges. Transfer the cookies to a wire rack and cool completely. Spread Espresso Frosting (below) on top of each cookie. Allow the frosting to set.

ESPRESSO FROSTING

INGREDIENTS

2	tablespoons unsalted butter, softened
1	cup powdered sugar
½	teaspoon ground cinnamon
1	teaspoon pure vanilla extract
1	tablespoon liquid java—made with espresso powder or use strongly brewed coffee, cooled

DIRECTIONS

Put all the ingredients into a medium bowl; beat with a mixer on low speed just until smooth.

ALMOND-CHOCOLATE CHIP COOKIES WITH AMARETTO FROSTING

*The original recipe uses ground almonds. To make life easier, I replaced the ground nuts with almond flour—it works perfectly. Use the liqueur again to make **Amaretto Chocolate Chip Cookies** (page 56).*

- Makes about 2½ dozen -

INGREDIENTS

Extra butter to grease the baking sheets

1 cup all-purpose flour

½ cup raw almond flour

½ teaspoon baking soda

¼ teaspoon salt

2 tablespoons unsalted butter, softened

2 tablespoons shortening, at room temperature

¼ cup granulated sugar

¾ cup firmly packed light-brown sugar

1 large egg

1 tablespoon amaretto liqueur

1 teaspoon pure almond extract

¼ cup semisweet chocolate chips

¼ cup coarsely chopped almonds

DIRECTIONS

Preheat the oven to 375 degrees F.

Lightly grease baking sheets (shiny-metal sheets work best). Set aside.

In a 1-quart bowl, sift together both flours, the baking soda, and salt; whisk briefly. Set aside.

In a large bowl and with a mixer on low speed, cream together the butter and shortening. Gradually add both sugars; beat until very well blended. Beat in the egg, liqueur, and extract. Use a wooden spoon to stir in the flour mixture in 4 parts. Stir in the chips and nuts. Set aside.

Prepare Amaretto Frosting (below). Set aside.

Drop dough by level tablespoons onto the prepared baking sheets, spacing about 2 inches apart. Bake for 10 minutes or until lightly browned. Transfer cookies to a wire rack. While still warm, use a pastry brush to spread frosting on top of each cookie. Cool completely and then brush with frosting again.

AMARETTO FROSTING

INGREDIENTS

2   ounces cream cheese, softened

1   cup powdered sugar

1   tablespoon amaretto liqueur

DIRECTIONS

Put the cream cheese, powdered sugar, and 1 tablespoon liqueur into a medium bowl. Beat with a mixer on low speed, adding additional liqueur as needed to reach a smooth and desirable consistency.

PECAN TARTLETS

A baby pecan pie—savor it in small bites. Streamline the recipe by using purchased refrigerated pie crusts (see Note below). If you like, lightly dust tartlets with powdered sugar for a lovely finish.

- Makes about 2 dozen -

CRUST

INGREDIENTS

1   cup all-purpose flour

½   cup (1 stick) cold unsalted butter, cut into bits

3   ounces cold cream cheese, cut into pieces

CRUST

DIRECTIONS

Put the flour into a medium bowl; sprinkle butter and cream cheese on top. With a pastry blender, cut the butter and cream cheese into the flour until the mixture is well combined. Roll level tablespoons of dough into 24 balls. Use floured fingertips to press balls evenly over the bottom and up the sides of 24 ungreased 1¾-inch mini-muffin pan cups.

FILLING

INGREDIENTS

⅔	cup chopped pecans, divided in half
1	large egg
1	teaspoon pure vanilla extract
¾	cup firmly packed light-brown sugar
1	tablespoon unsalted butter, melted

DIRECTIONS

Preheat the oven to 375 degrees F.

Distribute ⅓ cup nuts evenly among each cup of crust.

In a small bowl, whisk the filling ingredients—except pecans. Spoon about 1 teaspoon into each crust. Sprinkle with the remaining ⅓ cup nuts. (There will be extra filling; bake it in a custard cup—for you.)

Bake 25 minutes. (Place a baking sheet on the rack below the muffin pan to catch any bubbly-butter overflow.) Cool tartlets in the pan on a rack for a few minutes. While still warm, use a thin knife blade to loosen and lift them from the pan. Transfer to a wire rack and cool completely.

> **Note:** Instead of making crust, REFRIGERATED "JUST UN-ROLL & BAKE" PIE CRUSTS may be substituted. Use a 2¾-inch round cookie cutter to cut the crusts into 24 rounds. Fit the rounds into 24 mini-muffin pan cups.

ALMOST MOM'S APRICOT KOLACKY

Mom made yeast-dough kolacky; it was always a big project. Instead, I found this simpler recipe and stuck with it over the years. My homage to Mom is her twist of adding a generous sprinkle of chopped pecans. Other fillings like prune or cherry may be substituted, but apricot with pecans is just the best.

- Makes about 3 dozen –

INGREDIENTS

	Powdered sugar for dusting (about 2 tablespoons)
2	cups all-purpose flour
2	teaspoons baking powder
1	cup (2 sticks) unsalted butter, softened
6	ounces cream cheese, softened
1	can (12 ounces) apricot pastry filling
1½-2	cups chopped pecans

DIRECTIONS

Preheat the oven to 350 degrees F.

Into a medium bowl, sift the flour with the baking powder; whisk briefly. Set aside.

In a large bowl and with a mixer on low speed, cream the butter with the cream cheese until smoothly blended. Continuing on low speed, gradually beat in as much flour mixture as you can. Use a wooden spoon to stir in any remaining flour. Gather the dough into a disk. If the dough is very soft, refrigerate ½ to 1 hour until firm enough to roll out easily.

On a lightly floured surface, roll portions of dough to a ⅛-inch thickness. Cut with a 2½-inch scalloped or plain round cookie cutter; space 2 inches apart on ungreased baking sheets. Make an indentation with three fingers on each round. Fill with about 1 teaspoon filling; generously sprinkle with pecans.

Bake for 15 to 20 minutes or until the bottoms are light golden brown. Cool 5 minutes on the baking sheet and then transfer to a wire rack. Cool completely. Lightly dust with powdered sugar dredged through a fine-mesh sieve.

> **Note:** Use shiny-metal baking sheets for light-golden-brown bottoms. Absolutely avoid dark, non-stick sheets for this recipe. Note also, using a scalloped cookie cutter adds extra visual and textured appeal.

LINZER COOKIES

This recipe will push your skills; it requires a bit of labor but the rewards are great flavor and beauty.

- Makes about 5 dozen -

INGREDIENTS

Powdered sugar for dusting (about 2 tablespoons)

½ pound roasted unsalted hazelnuts (filberts)

1 cup unsalted butter (2 sticks), softened—plus more to grease the baking sheets

¾ cup granulated sugar

1 large egg

½ teaspoon salt

3 cups sifted all-purpose flour (sift first, then measure)

2 egg whites, lightly beaten

1 jar (10 ounces) seedless red raspberry jam

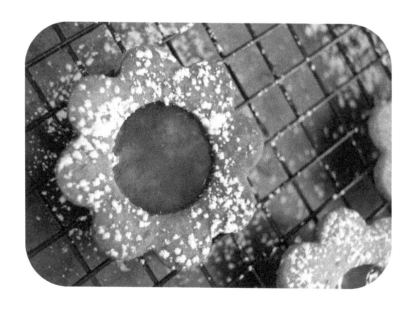

DIRECTIONS

Put the nuts into a clean dish towel and rub to loosen and remove most of the skins.

In a food processor (or see Note page 67), finely grind enough nuts to equal 2 cups. Set aside.

In a large bowl and with a mixer on medium speed, cream the butter until smooth, about 30 seconds. Gradually add the sugar and then beat until light and fluffy, 4 to 5 minutes. Beat in the egg and salt. Reduce speed to low. Add the flour in 4 parts. Use a wooden spoon to blend in the nuts. Shape the dough into a square and wrap tightly in saran. Refrigerate for at least 2 hours.

Preheat the oven to 375 degrees F.

Lightly grease shiny-metal baking sheets. Set aside.

On a lightly floured surface, roll portions of dough very thinly to less than a ⅛-inch thickness. Use a 2½-inch scalloped cookie cutter to cut out rounds from half the dough. Cut remaining dough into scalloped rounds with ½-inch "windows." Place whole rounds on prepared sheets and brush with egg whites, using a pastry brush. Place "windowed" rounds on separate sheets and bake separately.

Bake until just lightly browned, about 8 minutes (see Note below). Transfer the cookies to a wire rack and cool for 5 minutes.

Spread each full cookie with a scant teaspoon of jam; top with a "windowed" cookie. Cool completely. Dust with powdered sugar dredged through a fine-mesh sieve.

Note: The "windowed" rounds brown fast, so watch them very carefully. Shiny-metal baking sheets will be most helpful.

FLOURLESS COOKIES

Below are a dozen delicious, no-wheat-flour cookie alternatives.

FLOURLESS PEANUT BUTTER COOKIES

Known as 1-2-3 cookies, the original recipe uses one cup each of peanut butter and granulated sugar and just one egg. For a more refined flavor, I use brown sugar and add vanilla extract. Plus, baking soda improves the texture. Use shiny-metal baking sheets and the cookies will also have scrumptious light-golden-brown bottoms.

- Makes 4 dozen small or 2 dozen large cookies -

INGREDIENTS

1	cup creamy peanut butter
1	cup firmly packed light-brown sugar
1	large egg
½	teaspoon pure vanilla extract
½	teaspoon baking soda

DIRECTIONS

Preheat the oven to 350 degrees F.

In a large bowl and with a mixer on low speed, beat the peanut butter with the brown sugar until smoothly blended. Beat in the egg, extract, and baking soda.

Use either a 1-tablespoon measure for large cookies or a ½-tablespoon measure for small cookies. (If making both sizes at once, use separate sheets and bake separately.) Heap dough into the measuring spoon and level off at the rim with a butter knife. Scoop the dough out and drop onto ungreased baking sheets, spacing about 2 inches apart. Shape each mound of dough into a ball. Use a fork to flatten the balls to about a ⅜-inch thickness.

Bake large cookies for about 10 minutes; small cookies for about 7. Cool on the baking sheet until firm enough to move, 7 to 8 minutes. Transfer cookies to a wire rack and cool completely.

VARIATIONS

(1.) Garnish thoroughly cooled cookies with a scant drizzle of melted bitter or semi-sweet chocolate. (2.) Instead of flattening balls with a fork, press your thumb into the center to form a well. Fill with seedless red raspberry preserves, about ¼ teaspoon for small cookies and ½ teaspoon for large. Bake as above. Cool completely and then drizzle with melted chocolate.

FLOURLESS OAT & PEANUT BUTTER COOKIES

Make these cookies your own by including add-ins you love. Toss in a small handful of chocolate chips (milk or semisweet); hulled roasted sunflower seeds; pepitas (hulled pumpkin seeds); raisins; chopped dried cherries, apricots, or dates—whatever you like.

- Makes about 2½ dozen –

INGREDIENTS

2	tablespoons unsalted butter, softened
½	cup peanut butter
6	tablespoons granulated sugar
6	tablespoons firmly packed dark-brown sugar
1	large egg
½	teaspoon pure vanilla extract
½	teaspoon baking soda
1½	cups dry old-fashioned rolled oats (not quick-cooking or instant)
¼	to ½ cup salted or unsalted dry-roasted peanuts (and/or other add-ins)

DIRECTIONS

Preheat the oven to 350 degrees F.

In a large bowl and with a mixer on low speed, cream together the butter and peanut butter until smoothly blended. Add both sugars and then beat until thoroughly combined. Beat in the egg, extract, and baking soda until smooth and creamy. Use a wooden spoon to stir in the oats, nuts and any add-ins.

Use 1 level tablespoon of dough per cookie and drop onto ungreased baking sheets, spacing about 2 inches apart. Shape each mound of dough into a ball, and then flatten slightly with the bottom of a drinking glass, a fork, or your fingertips.

Bake for about 12 minutes or until set and the bottoms are golden. Cool cookies on the baking sheet until firm enough to move, about 3 minutes. Transfer to a wire rack and cool completely.

GLUTEN-FREE CHOCOLATE-BROWNIE COOKIES

These soft and chewy, dark-chocolaty cookies are fabulous. For best results, combine ingredients in the order given. Blend the wet ingredients first, and then mix in the dry ingredients in the manner specified. If you blend in the cocoa with a mixer, you will create a cocoa dust storm in your kitchen.

- Makes about 2½ dozen -

INGREDIENTS

	Parchment paper
	Walnut halves for garnish (optional)
¾	cup almond butter
1	large egg
⅓	cup 100% pure maple syrup
2	tablespoons melted coconut oil
1	teaspoon pure vanilla extract
1	tablespoon arrowroot powder
1	teaspoon baking soda
¼	cup natural (non-alkalized) unsweetened cocoa powder
2	ounces dark-bittersweet chocolate, coarsely chopped (a scant ½ cup)

DIRECTIONS

Preheat the oven to 350 degrees F.
Line baking sheets with parchment paper. Set aside.

In a large bowl combine the first 5 wet ingredients (almond butter through extract); beat with a mixer on low speed until smoothly blended. Add the arrowroot powder and baking soda; continue to beat until well combined. Use a rubber spatula to stir in the cocoa powder. Fold in the chopped chocolate.

Use 1 level tablespoon of mixture per cookie and drop onto the prepared baking sheets, spacing about 2 inches apart. If desired, place a walnut half on top of some cookies for variety.

Bake for 8 to 10 minutes or until the edges have set. (The cookies will appear soft but will firm up as they cool.) Cool cookies 10 minutes on the baking sheet. Transfer to a wire rack and cool completely.

> **Note:** For the dark chocolate, use one-half of a 4-ounce Ghirardelli bittersweet 60% cacao premium baking bar.

GLUTEN-FREE
LEMON-ALMOND COOKIES

Raw almond flour is the star ingredient in this recipe. The natural nut—in its skin—is finely ground to yield a flour with dark speckles in it. If you would like to use the ingredient in other no-wheat-flour recipes, see **Gluten-Free Coconut Drops** *(page 198) and* **My Favorite Granola Bars** *(page 212).*

- Makes about 20 cookies –

INGREDIENTS

	Parchment paper
	Whole and/or slivered almonds for garnish
2	cups raw almond flour
⅔-¾	cup granulated sugar, to taste
	Shaved zest from 1 small lemon*
½	tablespoon fresh lemon juice
1	egg white from a large egg
½	teaspoon pure vanilla extract

DIRECTIONS

Preheat the oven to 350 degrees F.

Line baking sheets with parchment paper. Set aside.

In a large bowl, thoroughly whisk the almond flour with the sugar and zest.

In a small bowl or cup, whisk together the juice, egg white, and extract; add to the flour mixture and stir with a rubber spatula until well combined.

Use 1 level tablespoon of dough per cookie and shape into balls. Space about 2 inches apart on the prepared baking sheets. Use your thumb to lightly press a well into each ball; fill with 1 whole or 2 slivered almonds.

Bake for 13 to 15 minutes for cookies that are slightly crunchy on the outside and chewy on the inside. Bake for 10 to 12 minutes for softer cookies. Thoroughly cool on a wire rack.

*See **Orange & Lemon Zest** (page XIII).

GLUTEN-FREE COCONUT DROPS

Maple syrup imparts a delicious complex sweetness, but also cause the cookies to be a bit sticky on the bottom. The stickiness is easily managed by eating the cookies chilled and licking fingertips often.

- Makes about 2 dozen -

INGREDIENTS

	Parchment paper
1	cup raw almond flour
½	teaspoon baking powder
¼	teaspoon salt
1½	cups sweetened flaked coconut
1	large egg
⅓	cup 100% pure maple syrup
2½	tablespoons canola or corn oil
1	teaspoon pure vanilla extract
¼	cup semisweet chocolate chips

DIRECTIONS

Preheat the oven to 350 degrees F.

Line baking sheets with parchment paper. Set aside.

Into a large bowl, sift the almond flour, baking powder, and salt. Stir in the coconut. Set aside.

In a medium bowl, whisk the egg with the syrup, oil, and extract. Add the wet ingredients to the dry ingredients all at once; stir together with a rubber spatula. Stir in the chocolate chips.

Drop level tablespoons of the mixture onto the prepared baking sheets, spacing about 2 inches apart.

Bake for 15 to 17 minutes or until golden brown. Place the baking sheets on a wire rack and let the cookies cool on the sheet. Peel cookies off the parchment paper when completely cooled.

SORGHUM MOLASSES COOKIES

This recipe produces a spicy, soft and chewy cookie that is really quite delectable. Find sorghum flour and xanthan gum in health food stores. For more about these ingredients, see page X. If you would like to use the flour and gum in other recipes, see **Sorghum Coconut-Oatmeal Cookies** *(page 202) and* **Sorghum Banana-Walnut Cookies** *(page 204).*

- Makes about 33 cookies –

INGREDIENTS

	Parchment paper	¼	teaspoon salt
	About ½ cup turbinado (raw) sugar	4	tablespoons unsalted butter, softened
2	cups sorghum flour	¾	cup firmly packed light-brown sugar
2	teaspoons ground cinnamon	1	large egg
½	teaspoon ground ginger	¼	cup molasses
½	teaspoon xanthan gum	½	teaspoon pure vanilla extract
½	teaspoon baking soda		

DIRECTIONS

Into a medium bowl, sift the first 6 dry ingredients (sorghum flour through salt); whisk briefly. Set aside.

In a large bowl and with a mixer on low speed, cream together the butter and brown sugar. Beat in the egg, molasses, and extract. Continuing on low speed, beat in the dry ingredients in 4 or 5 parts. (The dough will be very soft.) Cover the bowl with saran and refrigerate for at least 1 hour or more.

Preheat the oven to 350 degrees F.

Line baking sheets with parchment paper.

Put the turbinado sugar into a small shallow bowl.

Keeping the dough cold and working with small portions, use 1 level tablespoon of dough per cookie and shape into balls. Roll each ball in the turbinado sugar to coat allover. Space about 2 inches apart on the prepared baking sheets.

Bake for 8 to 10 minutes or until just set. Let the cookies cool on the baking sheet until firm enough to move, about 3 minutes. Transfer to a wire rack and cool completely.

SORGHUM COCONUT-OATMEAL COOKIES

Chewy, and with a clean sweet flavor, this cookie is worth making even if you're not avoiding wheat flour. Raisins taste great with the coconut and pecans, but chopped dates, dried chopped apricots, or dried cranberries work well here, too.

- Makes about 3 dozen -

INGREDIENTS

Parchment paper

⅔ cup sorghum flour

1 tablespoon cornstarch

½ teaspoon xanthan gum

½ teaspoon baking powder

¼ teaspoon salt

½ cup (1 stick) unsalted butter, softened

½ cup firmly packed light-brown sugar

1 large egg

½ teaspoon pure vanilla extract

¼ cup honey

1 cup dry old-fashioned rolled oats (not quick-cooking or instant)

½ cup sweetened flaked coconut

¼ cup coarsely chopped pecans

¼ cup raisins

DIRECTIONS

Preheat the oven to 350 degrees F.

Line baking sheets with parchment paper. Set aside.

Into a 1-quart bowl, sift the first 5 dry ingredients (sorghum flour through salt); whisk briefly. Set aside.

In a large bowl and with a mixer on low speed, cream the butter. Gradually add the brown sugar and then beat until very well blended. Beat in the egg, extract, and honey. Continuing on low speed, add the sorghum-flour mixture in 3 parts, beating until smoothly blended. Use a rubber spatula or wooden spoon to stir in the oats, coconut, nuts, and raisins.

Drop the dough by level tablespoons onto the prepared baking sheets, spacing about 2 inches apart.

Bake for about 12 minutes or until browned around the edges. Cool 5 minutes on the baking sheet. Transfer cookies to a wire rack and cool completely.

SORGHUM BANANA-WALNUT COOKIES

A touch of nutmeg pairs beautifully with the banana flavor, and walnuts add crunchiness. The cookies are slightly sugary-crisp on top; soft and cake-like on the inside. They taste best when freshly baked.

- Makes about 2 dozen –

INGREDIENTS

Extra butter to grease the baking sheets

About 1½ tablespoons granulated sugar to flatten cookies

1   cup sorghum flour

¼   teaspoon xanthan gum

¼   teaspoon baking soda

⅛   teaspoon ground nutmeg

⅛   teaspoon salt

2   tablespoons unsalted butter, softened

¼   cup firmly packed light-brown sugar

1   egg white from a large egg

½   teaspoon pure vanilla extract

½   cup mashed ripe banana (about 1 medium)

½   cup dry quick-cooking rolled oats (not instant or old-fashioned)

½   cup coarsely chopped walnuts

DIRECTIONS

Preheat the oven to 350 degrees F.

Lightly grease baking sheets. Set aside.

Into a 1-quart bowl, sift the first 5 dry ingredients (sorghum flour through salt); whisk briefly. Set aside.

In a large bowl and with a wooden spoon, cream together the butter and brown sugar. Vigorously beat in the egg white and extract; beat in the banana. Use a rubber spatula to stir in the sorghum-flour mixture in 3 parts, stirring in each addition just until incorporated. Fold in the oats and nuts.

Put the granulated sugar into a small bowl. Drop the dough by level tablespoons onto the prepared baking sheets, spacing about 2 inches apart. Flatten to about a ⅜-inch thickness with the greased bottom of a glass dipped into the granulated sugar.

Bake for 10 to 12 minutes or until lightly browned around the edges and on the bottoms. Cool 2 to 3 minutes on the baking sheet. Transfer cookies to a wire rack and cool completely.

COCONUT MERINGUES

These meringues are tender, light and especially delicious when made with just a little vanilla extract. The original recipe uses peppermint extract and includes chocolate chips—do this, if you like. However, the cookie is sublime in its most uncomplicated form. Voluminous beaten egg whites are essential for the success of this recipe (see Note below).

- Makes about 4 dozen -

INGREDIENTS

	Parchment paper
3	egg whites from large eggs
¼	teaspoon cream of tartar
⅛	teaspoon salt
¾	cup granulated sugar
¼	teaspoon pure vanilla extract
2	cups sweetened flaked coconut

DIRECTIONS

Have all ingredients at room temperature.

Position a rack in the upper third of the oven; preheat to 300 degrees F.

Line 2 baking sheets with parchment paper. Set aside.

In a 1½-quart bowl and with a mixer on medium speed, beat the egg whites with the cream of tartar and salt until foamy. Increase speed to high and gradually beat in the sugar, 1 tablespoon at a time.

Continue beating until the whites are stiff and glossy, 4 to 5 minutes more. Scrape the mixture into a large bowl; fold in the extract and coconut with a rubber spatula.

Drop level tablespoons of batter onto the prepared baking sheets, spacing about 1 to 1½ inches apart.

Bake for 25 minutes or until just lightly browned. (You may bake both sheets at the same time.) Cool the meringues on the baking sheets for 10 minutes. Gently remove from the paper and cool completely.

Note: TO PRODUCE WELL BEATEN EGG WHITES, use a bowl and beaters that are completely free of detergent and fat, and avoid plastic bowls which retain a greasy film. Fat prevents the whites from whipping properly. To eliminate all fat, wipe the bowl and beaters with white vinegar, rinse and dry well. To avoid spoiling all the egg whites in case a fatty yolk breaks, separate them one at a time into a smaller bowl, then add to the mixing bowl. Cream of tartar (an acidic powder) stabilizes the whites and adds volume. If you have none on hand, use a dash of lemon juice.

COCOA MERINGUE KISSES

Petit meringues offer a tasty smooch on the lips when dusted with cocoa powder.

Don't shy away from the warm-water method used in the recipe below. It takes out the guesswork of when to start and how fast to add the sugar to the egg whites. It produces a perfect meringue.

- Makes about 50 meringues –

INGREDIENTS

Parchment paper

Extra cocoa powder for dusting (2 to 3 teaspoons), more if coating allover

2	egg whites from large eggs
¼	teaspoon cream of tartar
1	teaspoon pure vanilla extract
½	cup fine granulated sugar
3	tablespoons natural (non-alkalized) unsweetened cocoa powder

DIRECTIONS

Preheat the oven to 225 degrees F.

Line 2 large baking sheets with parchment paper. Set aside.

In a 2-quart heatproof bowl, whisk the egg whites with the cream of tartar, vanilla extract, and sugar. To thoroughly dissolve the sugar, set the bowl into a skillet of gently simmering water and whisk until the whites are warm to the touch, not hot. Rub a bit of the mixture between fingers; if it doesn't feel gritty, the sugar is dissolved. Remove bowl from the skillet and beat with a mixer on high speed until the whites are stiff, about 5 minutes. Sift 3 tablespoons cocoa powder over the surface; gently fold into the meringue with a rubber spatula.

Using a heaping teaspoon of meringue for each cookie, drop the batter onto the prepared baking sheets, spacing about 2 inches apart. Lightly dust with extra cocoa powder dredged through a fine-mesh sieve.

Bake both sheets at once for 1 hour. Turn the heat off and allow meringues to dry in the oven until completely cool, about 2 hours.

Note: If desired, put finished meringues into a sturdy zipper-top bag, add extra cocoa powder and gently shake to thoroughly cover allover. Write the date on the bag and the meringues will be perfectly stored. They will stay crisp for several weeks at room temperature. Alternatively, simply store meringues in an airtight, moisture-proof container.

NO-BAKE PEANUT BUTTER
OAT SQUARES

Here's a no-flour, cereal-based recipe that won't heat up your kitchen. I enjoy eating these crispy squares during the hot summer months. They crumble easily at room temperature, so it's best to eat them frozen. You will love the delicious peanut butter-toffee flavor. Be sure to use dark-brown sugar.

- Makes about 16 squares -

INGREDIENTS

Cooking spray

Wax paper

1½ cups dry old-fashioned rolled oats (not instant or quick-cooking)

1 cup crisp rice cereal

½ cup roughly chopped pecans

¼ cup dark raisins or chopped dates (my favorite is dates)

¼ cup creamy peanut butter

¼ cup honey

¼ cup firmly packed dark-brown sugar

DIRECTIONS

Lightly coat a 9-inch square pan with cooking spray. Set aside.

In a large bowl, thoroughly combine the first 4 ingredients (oats through raisins).

In a 1½-quart sauce pan over low heat, stir the peanut butter with the honey until melted. Add the brown sugar and bring to a bubbly simmer over medium heat, stirring constantly, just until the sugar is dissolved and the mixture is blended. Pour over the dry ingredients all at once; immediately stir to quickly and thoroughly combine.

Scrape the mixture into the prepared pan; spread and press evenly into a flat layer with a rubber spatula. Cool at room temperature until thoroughly cooled and set.

Invert onto a wax-paper-lined cutting surface and cut into squares. (The squares will be quite soft but will firm-up nicely when frozen.) Place squares in a flat-airtight container between layers of wax paper or wrap individually in saran, as you like.

Note: Store in the freezer, and eat the squares while still frozen.

MY FAVORITE GRANOLA BARS

Cinnamon and clove impart spicy flavor—and sumptuous aroma—to these soft and chewy oatmeal bars. They are so amazingly delicious, I keep a batch in the freezer for myself. They thaw in minutes and are always available. The original recipe uses whole-wheat flour, but the flavor is remarkably improved with almond flour (finely ground almonds). You may use whole-wheat flour if desired, (see Note below).

- Makes about 8 bars –

INGREDIENTS

	Cooking spray	½	cup canola or corn oil
¾	cup raw almond flour (or whole-wheat flour)	1	large egg
¾	teaspoon ground cinnamon	1	cup dry old-fashioned rolled oats (not instant or quick-cooking)
⅛	teaspoon ground cloves		
½	teaspoon baking soda	½	cup chopped dates
½	cup firmly packed light-brown sugar	½	cup coarsely chopped walnuts

DIRECTIONS

Preheat the oven to 350 degrees F.

Lightly coat an 8-inch square pan with cooking spray. Set aside.

Into a 1-quart bowl, sift the almond flour, cinnamon, cloves, and baking soda; whisk briefly. Set aside.

In a large bowl, whisk together the brown sugar, oil and egg until smoothly blended. Use a wooden spoon to stir in the almond-flour mixture in 3 parts. Stir in the oats; stir in dates and nuts. With a sturdy rubber spatula, spread and pat the dough evenly into the prepared pan.

Bake for 20 to 25 minutes or until the center is set but not firm. Cool completely on a wire rack. Cut into bars, including some outer edge on each piece (the edges are delicious). Place bars in a flat-airtight container between layers of saran, or wrap individually. If desired, store in the freezer.

> **Note:** With whole-wheat flour, shorter baking time is required—bake for only about 15 minutes. Also, the ingredients may be doubled and baked in a 15x10x1-inch jelly roll pan for about 17 minutes. Doubling ingredients does not work out as well when using almond flour.

INDEX

A

B

Z
Zest

ACKNOWLEDGEMENTS

Thank you to my husband Jeff who always believes in me and my ability to write a book.

I am deeply grateful to Julio Aranda. Without his computer expertise I would be at a total loss in today's technology.

My heartfelt gratitude goes out to everyone I know, including all my family, friends, neighbors and coworkers—present and past. I'm fortunate to have had all of you in my life.

I thank all the gentle spirits of nature that deeply touch me every day with quiet inspiration. I thank the presence that beats my heart and breathes air into my lungs; its energy is here.

I LOVE ALL OF YOU.

And, thank you to my beloved dog Pepper—my loyal child-hood friend and protector.

ABOUT ATMOSPHERE PRESS

Atmosphere Press is an independent, full-service publisher for excellent books in all genres and for all audiences. Learn more about what we do at atmospherepress.com.

We encourage you to check out some of Atmosphere's latest releases, which are available at Amazon.com and via order from your local bookstore:

The Great Unfixables, by Neil Taylor

Soused at the Manor House, by Brian Crawford

Portal or Hole: Meditations on Art, Religion, Race And The Pandemic, by Pamela M. Connell

A Walk Through the Wilderness, by Dan Conger

The House at 104: Memoir of a Childhood, by Anne Hegnauer

A Short History of Newton Hall, Chester, by Chris Fozzard

Serial Love: When Happily Ever After... Isn't, by Kathy Kay

Sit-Ins, Drive-Ins and Uncle Sam, by Bill Slawter

Black Water and Tulips, by Sara Mansfield Taber

Ghosted: Dating & Other Paramoural Experiences, by Jana Eisenstein

Walking with Fay: My Mother's Uncharted Path into Dementia, by Carolyn Testa

FLAWED HOUSES of FOUR SEASONS, by James Morris

Word for New Weddings, by David Glusker and Thom Blackstone

It's Really All about Collaboration and Creativity! A Textbook and Self-Study Guide for the Instrumental Music Ensemble Conductor, by John F. Colson

A Life of Obstructions, by Rob Penfield

Troubled Skies Over Quaker Hill: A Search for the Truth, by Lessie Auletti

ABOUT THE AUTHOR

Marilyn Alice Tuckman is a sensory food taster and a former quality control and laboratory technician for a major bakery and condiment manufacturer.

She is a graduate of Elmhurst University with a B.S. in Psychology, and she lives with her husband Jeff in Elk Grove Village, Illinois. They share their home with two tabby cats— brother and sister Paxon and Pippen.

Tuckman is also the author of *For the Love of Pumpkins* (a cookbook).